# Vision for the Near Sighted

Joe Sigwarth

River Lights Publishing Services
1098 Main Street
Dubuque, IA 52001
www.rlb2e.com

Copyright © 2012 by Joe Sigwarth. All rights reserved.

ISBN: 978-0-9831240-3-0

Printed in the United States of America.

# Contents

**Preface**  v

**Chapter 1** Embrace His Grace ..................... 1

**Chapter 2** Want Life to Be Nice? Here's Some Advice .......................... 35

**Chapter 3** I Do Declare ........................... 75

**Chapter 4** Poetic Lines to Loves of Mine ..... 87

**Final Words**  103

# Preface

My name is Joe Sigwarth. I am a 66 year old farmer and have lived in Balltown, Iowa, my whole life. This book presents some profound thoughts with simple observations for your consideration. There are also a few anecdotes and sayings of my father and family. Some poems are offered for a light-hearted story of life. I hope this mix is enjoyable for all who take the time to read it. I am a graduate of St. Francis Catholic School, which was an eight grade elementary school. I still milk dairy cows each day at the century-plus homestead Sigwarth farm. Please ponder the experiences of my humble life.

## The Golden Years

It seems like yesterday I was actively farming, milking cows. It seems like the day before, I was a parent to five children, guiding them on their way, and also a husband to a lovely wife; like the day before that, I was a lonely teenager and young adult searching for purpose. It seems like the day before that, I was a secure, confident child with lots of family around me. So what lies ahead tomorrow, now that I'm retired and a senior citizen? This is time to resolve any issues I may have. This is time to love and nourish the many grandchildren we have been blessed with. This is time to build and grow a happier and peaceful tomorrow. The issue most of us face is one of forgiveness. The asking for and giving of it are both difficult and rewarding. Another area is finding the true love God gives us, and communicating it to others in a way they understand and embrace. Some call this time in life "the Golden Years." It actually is more valuable than gold if you use the opportunity to look deep into one's self, and resolve what needs to be resolved, and to engage in a life of love for everyone to participate in.

# Tomorrow

After a couple of cocktails, and some spiritual conversation, I have the thought that I want to go, but don't want to let go. Why? Too many unfinished thoughts and resolutions, too many unanswered questions. Why not here instead of there? This is our time to learn and grow. Yet there is a feeling of closeness and deliverance from the issues that haunt us. This is near, and welcomed. Yet, I want to share what I've learned and experienced, and what God has shown me. It is all connected, and all is beautiful. I need time to put this in words and feelings to let everyone know: This is what *tomorrow* is all about.

Joe Sigwarth<br>May 2012

# 1 | Embrace His Grace

## John

One of the first questions in the old Baltimore Catechism was, "Why were we created?" The given answer was "to know, love, and serve the Lord in this life and the next." Certainly John achieved all three in his relatively short stay with all of us. John and John's spirit were special and unique when he arrived, were evident in the magnitude of his life and remain so for all eternity. John and his life require them to be celebrated and not mourned—thankful for his many gifts, and not resentful that we wanted more. John's life was large and I'm sure he wants his family and acquaintances to be as large as the universe in accepting the timing of his death. Everyone he touched is better for it. Let us all accept his life with us and his sudden passing as part of a much larger plan and will that started with his creation. Look past ourselves and see the light that John's life shines so brightly—today and always.

## I'll Be There

This title of a popular song a few years ago reminds me of the everlasting presence of God. And what comes with God's presence? The endless love for now and eternity, which will give us life forever. Let me use a few descriptive words to identify God's love and how we feel it. First, the warmth is humanly comparable to the powerful warmth of the sun, which sustains life on Earth. Another is security. He will protect us from all evil and harm. You might say, "Why is there so much crime and suffering?" God will protect us from spiritual evil and harm if we allow Him to. He certainly is our first responder here in life. He will be our counselor and advisor because He listens to our innermost thoughts and feelings. And if we are open to His answers, they will be known and received by us. God's covenant with us will never expire, so it is like an eternal guarantee of His love and trust. God is there for us, so let us be there with Him.

### Life's Destination

I came here naked with empty hand.
Then of course came the demand
To prosper and gather material goods.
They will fade someday, that's understood.
What will remain are the deeds of love.
That is what a lifetime is built of.
My body is failing and worn out.
It says to me, "Please let me out."
It is God's will to now say goodbye.
Is it my will also? Yes, say I.
To all who know me, please don't stress.
I'm living on, just changing my address.

## Trust

This word "trust" has a very strong meaning to most of us, and it surely should. It is one of the most important qualities of our lives. It starts with the little things in our daily lives such as trusting that the food we eat will nourish us, the clothing we wear will keep us warm, and the pilot will give us a safe trip as we board an airplane. Those things are nothing compared to the trust that is necessary in a personal relationship. I would say it is the foundation needed for a lasting and loving togetherness we search for with one another. Without a foundation, it is difficult to build. We give freely of ourselves when we trust the person we are giving to. This is true freedom. Some of the building components are honesty, compassion, generosity, companionship, and even intimacy. Above all, we must trust ourselves to trust others. We have to draw on our strengths, our confidence, and our self-respect. That is why I always say with total conviction, "Trust in the Lord." He will never let us down or disappoint us.

## The Wait

Much of our life we have to wait.
Even after hurrying so we aren't late.
Take a number and wait your turn.
When will we ever learn
That life has enough time for all our needs.
Make little of the waiting game and focus on deeds.
Because while we are doing
We are not busy stewing.
As you wait, do something positive.
You will find a better way to live.
Let's see if we can't do much more
Before the final day we wait all our life for.

## Opportunity

This human life is not a test. Rather, it is a learning opportunity.

We are invited to experience and retain the love and goodness of our Creator. As someone said, "It is not how we get to God but how God comes to us." To consume this love to the fullest is an eternal journey with Jesus Christ as our guide. His love is endless and so is our partaking of it.

Early in our lives we are taught to look toward ourselves. Do our parents approve of us? In school, how well we score on our tests determines our self worth. We start to perform for the approval of others, and not to love and serve others. As we are busy looking and appraising our accomplishments, it is very easy and natural to become selfish.

Unless we learn to love and serve others, we become a slave to others and their expectations. Many people spend a lifetime attempting to satisfy these expectations and never use their God-given, natural, creative ability and talents. The use of these will bring personal satisfaction and happiness and a wonderful relationship with God's total Creation.

## Faith, Hope, Love

Faith is a tremendous gift of God. Faith is nothing more than being aware of and accepting God's Creation. Also, I might add, it is nothing less. To many people, this identification is very difficult to comprehend; therefore, this will leave us with doubts, fears, and anxieties. We humans are given so many gifts like faith from God, but many of these gifts are not accepted or enjoyed. They are set aside in a waiting position.

In simple terms, faith is believing what is actually there. Faith brings confidence, security and a wholeness that we are both born with and constantly need to maintain. It is the opposite of fear—it is fear turned upside down.

Let us proclaim the mystery of faith (words spoken in our Mass liturgy). I'd like to explore the word "mystery." Usually, it means something we don't understand. Understanding the how and why about something isn't as important as understanding the fact that it exists and that we can choose to allow ourselves to accept it. Again, this describes faith. So, if we understand faith, I ask the question, "Is faith really a mystery?"

Hope is a side effect of faith. When you choose to believe what is actually there, hope becomes your wish or prayer. A prayer to the future and to be a part of God's will and plan. We hope for good health and healing when it isn't there. This is true in a physical and in a spiritual state. We are born in good health in both states, as we start life as partners with God. Our hope is to return home after this human life to once again be perfect in God's union. Hope is beneficial in that it helps and leads us to do the living part of our lives.

Here is where love comes in. To love is God's will and plan and our instruction to carry out. The whole digestion of life is centered around our ability to love one another as He loves us. This is the wonderful task and invitation we are assigned the minute we are born. I have never understood why we take a task so simple and make it so difficult.

Loving has all the rewards and effect that it promises. Love is a slam dunk and scores the goal of uniting with our Lord in this life and all eternity. When asked what is the opposite of love, most people will answer that it is hate. I disagree with that answer, as I believe it to be selfishness. Some will say, "I did this kind and loving thing for someone else, therefore I must love them." This may be true, and it may not, depending on the motive for doing it. If it is done to satisfy self and possibly gain a return from this act, we have selfishness. A priest in a homily that I once heard stated, "There is no greater sin than to use another human being for your own personal gain." So, conditional love is not love at all. It is really an act of selfishness. Love with no conditions given freely is true love. So love is what one gives to a relationship and not what one takes. It is right to receive love given rather than to take it.

## Joy of Christmas

The joy of Christmas is so neat.
The Bethlehem scene was an extraordinary feat.
When divine and human came together as one
In the birth of God's only begotten Son.
The rest of His life is for history
To study and learn and see His glory.
For as we live each day, keep in mind
The joy of Jesus is there for all to find.

## Heritage

What does "heritage" mean to us and how much does it mean? To me, it is the true meaning of home. Our first earthly home is our mother's womb and is very comfortable. Once we are born, we inherit the spiritual qualities given to us by our Creator and the human genes given to us by our biological parents. Now it is our responsibility to use and enjoy these gifts for good and happiness.

It is important to be *aware* of what they are and *allow* them to be nourished and grown throughout our lifetime. This is not always easy because of all the stimuli, attraction and temptation of a selfish humanity who cherishes the self more than the gifts that were given to us.

Be focused on the *aware* and *allow* aspects and you will see the love of God all around you. So, when I prepare to take my last breath, I will be looking forward to pulling into the driveway of my original spiritual home, with all the comfort, peace, and love that is there for me. By teaching this to others, we can pass on a legacy to those who are willing to learn.

## Awareness

The more one understands in life, the more frustrated one also becomes. Not so much as the lack of understanding we see exhibited in lots of other people, but rather the unwillingness to try to understand. This is understandable because if one sees a situation clearly, often it requires honesty and action on their part. This also usually requires self-sacrifice.

Now we circle back to the "unwilling" word. If we love ourselves more than the other person, this is difficult. If we love each other equally, then it becomes an extension of our well-being and good. We can allow ourselves to be raised to Christ consciousness or choose to wait for a future invitation or calling and, be assured, you have the lifetime of eternity to reach this complete and ultimate goal.

The converse of not caring to understand leaves us in a limbo state of being for which none of us admits to be striving. So, continue to see what you can see, feel what you allow to feel, and understand what you dare to understand for your own complete and total happiness, which is full admission and acknowledgement of being a Christ son or daughter of God the Father.

## Time

The most used word in the world.
As each second, minute, and hour are unfurled
It is looked at and watched all day long
By everyone in population's throng.
But stop and think, there is no such thing
Because it doesn't end or begin.
We measure something that isn't really there.
It always was, and will always be, just like air.
To be used to get people where they want to go
On a table of schedules, don't you know?
So it has some merit in all life's scheme.
Its use is daily, even for dreams.
Be thankful for this necessity that doesn't exist
For without it, there'd be nothing to wear on our wrist.

## Pride

What is pride and is it good or bad for us? I suggest it can be both if we understand pride in its true meaning. We should all be proud that we are children of God, created out of pure love. This makes us very worthwhile and precious. To be proud of this truth is very good and beneficial for us.

*To be proud of the "self" as being superior to others, whether, through status, wealth, or accomplishment is false and selfish.* The attitude of, "look who I am, and what I've done" is harmful and bad for us. It gives ourselves the sole credit for all of this, when nothing is possible without God's involvement. The ability we all possess and use came to us from our Creator and we proudly and responsibly used it for human good.

Pride only in ourselves literally makes ourselves a false idol as we continue to worship ourselves. When this becomes excessive, we refuse to admit mistakes or failings and never learn the lesson of forgiveness. Humility is the antidote to false pride and it is realized when we understand that each of us is a central part of God's creative plan or will.

So, when we face big decisions in life, do we choose to follow God's will (which, by the way, is always revealed to us if we look for it) or do we follow our own mind and its sometimes stubborn tantrum approach? One choice has acceptable long term results while the other leads to inner pain and suffering.

## Tomorrow

It is the most talked about day that really never arrives, because there is always another one daily. I believe if we would live the moment with as much energy as we do planning tomorrow we would be much more productive in our lives. Often what we do right now will affect tomorrow greatly. Short term actions produce long term results.

In perspective, what and how we live now will grow into our eternal tomorrow. When we pass from this human life, our tomorrow will finally and ultimately arrive. I'm convinced how we live our daily lives and our relationships with others will lead to a level of happiness and joy and fulfillment of our eternity. We can then forever partake of the love of God, because we chose to receive it in this life.

It is good to reflect on our actions daily in order to maximize the totality of God's love. There is nothing greater and is offered freely to all of us. It is up to each one of us to accept it and allow it into our hearts. Go for it!

## Grace and Blessings

The other day I asked myself this question: How many more good people and events will God send to me? It was while we were having a large family gathering with good people, food, conversation, and merriment. The answer came to me quickly. God is sending Himself to me through these beautiful people and all the senses I am able to enjoy. Not only does He send joy and happiness, He also sends many messages to me and all of the family. It is very important and wise for us to listen to these, and also to enjoy the good times we are able to taste. His message is that we deserve all of this, so be grateful and thankful, and share them with everyone. So, really these gifts are sent to all and not just me. Take time to enjoy these feelings and to retain the messages so they may live on. As the refrain in a hymn says, "Taste and see the goodness of the Lord."

## Angels

I met an angel today without wings.
She had a personality that beautifully sings.
These creatures seem so rare
But if you look, you'll see they are there.
A calm demeanor and a pleasant smile.
A person willing to walk the extra mile
To make others happy and content.
To bring joy and merriment
To everyone she meets on a daily basis.
These angel people are a true oasis
In a desert of doubt and sadness.
They bring confidence and gladness.
Also a spirit of goodness and love.
Showered on us from God above.
Be thankful for this heavenly gift.
For all of us who see them feel a fantastic lift.

## The Mirror

Many of us take time to look in a mirror quite often. Men look to see if they still have thick hair on their heads and if they may be turning gray. Women look to apply makeup of every kind to accent their beauty and also to style their hair in an attractive fashion. Of course, we must look at our body shape to assess weight gain or loss- and where. Another purpose of a mirror is to reflect on our life and how we are living it. Are you pleased with who and what you see? Do you like this guy or girl or could you improve your life's situation? After considering those questions, how about gazing into the mirror of your soul? Now we may see what is or isn't burning inside of us. Is it love, compassion, forgiveness, trust, and peace, or is it hatred, selfishness, bitterness, doubt, and unrest? Usually there is a mixture of these characteristics, some learned, some not. Are we seeing a lifestyle as Jesus taught us, "Come follow me," or are we observing a struggle with the limitations of the human body and mind alone? Remove the limits and allow yourself to see God within your soul where He resides in each and every one of us.

## Creation

A lot of articles of late address "creation." I just read an opinion that we humans are all co-creators with God. I see each one of us as an important and necessary element or cell of every living part of creation. I see it as an ongoing and evolving process that never ends. "I am the Alpha and the Omega."

Hence, we have eternity. We are all the part of every cell that is given new life and also part of every cell that passes on. The constant symphony of creation is so vast and yet so simple by the design of the Master. As my first pastor said of this human life, "We are just passing through." We see life's creation in every plant and tree as they die to new seed and new continuance. Creation is one concept that is truly all inclusive. This is where renewal and resurrection are constant. We humans can change or direct the timing in some of these creative events, but never the formula or process of them. This leads us to our spiritual place in all of this.

Most of us believe in a heaven or reward for our human life. I see this place as where you arrive when you have become totally aware of God's creation and existence in it. Thus, heaven is definitely possible to be here on Earth at any given moment for each of us. When we live in cooperation with God's creation, our goal will have been achieved. And the beauty of that is you can now share this with all mankind.

So, let us search for awareness in every breath that we take, and every beauty and manifestation of God through His creation. This is our reward or fulfillment for the opportunity of our human life and spiritual existence. Praise be to God.

One of the first questions in the Baltimore catechism in first grade of school was, "Why were we created?" The answer: To know, love, and serve the Lord in this life, and to be with Him in the next life. That was sixty years ago for me, but it is still powerful today. Once we realize where God exists, and we see the manifestation and beauty in all of His creation, we have learned or allowed ourselves to know God.

Someone once asked me, "When do you know when you have found God?" I replied, "When you have no more need to ask." To know God is to love Him as He *is* love. This is profound, but not complicated. Rather it is simple and inclusive. The "serve" part is whenever we love someone, we serve them by our actions of love and togetherness or oneness.

Our next life is our first life being continued for eternity. God knew us before we were created, so how could we not know Him? The only way would be to refuse or deny His love and remain in a state of emptiness. This would be hell.

## The Who

Who do you believe?
Who will not deceive.
The One who came to show
How life is meant to go.
We are always looking far and wide
For the who, who will help us decide.
The answer always lies within
For we are the ones who allow what comes in.
Allow Jesus in and look no longer.
Our faith will make us much stronger.
The questions in us will no longer quiver.
Christ the Lord alone will deliver.

## Is That All There Is?

How many people come to a stage in their lives when they ask themselves this question? For lots of us it is when we are ready for retirement and feel unfulfilled. For others it is when they enter a new relationship or new job, and soon there is this feeling of boredom and monotony. Of course, there is an answer to this old, old question. The is that is missing is the spiritual side of life, which many are too busy to explore, much less find. The possessions become empty in value because they are empty in real value—spiritual value.

Well, what should you do about it? Open your heart and your mind to love others, rather than love what you own or have physically built. It is never too late to open yourself to the spirit of God. God has no limitations or boundaries as material things do. God's creation is the "all" that you haven't bothered to see before. This "all" is the people around us, and those we touch throughout our lifetimes. It is also the nature that nourishes us and sustains us. So, when we get our priorities in proper order, we will live in the spirit of God and be satisfied forever.

## Our Father

In our society today, psychologists and psychiatrists are working full schedules with people who are in one or more unhappy relationships. Many of these include parents who have problems relating in a happy manner with their children. I feel very often this situation is a result of not having resolved certain issues with their fathers. It seems it is a natural instinct to have approval from Dad. It isn't usually what one or the other did, sometimes it is what they didn't do.

Learning to communicate and express your feelings with children is of the utmost importance. It is also important to allow the children the same privilege. I realize that many children do not have a father to relate with, so the same will apply to the mother in this case.

Please break the generational cycle of this pattern by reaching out to fathers and parents while they are still with us. On the spiritual level, let us all do this with our Creator Father. The one that begins the Lord's Prayer, "Our Father, Who art in heaven," is waiting for us to find His approval by how we live a loving life in the now.

## Lost and Found

A popular hymn has a line, "I once was lost, but now I am found." This line has always intrigued me because we have all experienced some degree of this in our lives. Examples come to mind: A child who wandered away from parents and was quite scared until they find each other; when a decision or crossroads comes in life and is not easily solved or sure until we make a commitment to accept and live with it. The two words that appear important here are "now" and "found." I believe we find answers in the now and what is actual and truthful is now seen by us as a clear path. To me the greatest find is when we find ourselves and our true identity as a child of God. We were never lost by our Creator and Source, but we have a need and instinct to find that Being. We must find our spirit hidden in all the human identification that has led us to feel lost.

Isn't it ironic that we can only find our spirit in the "now" and not in the past or future? Those places are all part of our imagination and our spent energy that was following a selfish distraction that is our human ego. Once we transform from the ego shell or container we will find ourselves in the very real sense of who we really are spiritually. Once we find ourselves, there are no limitations to how close we can become to our beginning which began with our creation as a child of God.

## Who We Are

Many people struggle with who they are.
Where did they come from, near or far?
It wasn't a planet far away.
It was from God's hand and we're here to stay
Life is now forever for us to learn and grow.
You may ask "Why," because God planned it so.
We all got a name and a human start
But God wants always to live in our heart.
We are given a free will to choose our direction.
Always remember to live with affection
For those who surround us here on Earth.
As well as our heavenly Father who gave us self-worth.
So back to the question of who we are.
In God's whole creation we are one human star.
As individual, shining and as bright
As any of those shown to us at night.
You live each day, you are meant to have bliss.
When you believe in God's gift, nothing can challenge this.
Live in the here and the now, and eternity will always be.
When we go back to where we came, the who we are
will be easy to see.

## In the Groove

There are times in our lives when everything, or at least a situation, seems to be and feel satisfying and almost perfect. Some call it chemistry, others euphoria, or the alignment of the stars. When we are in the groove, we feel so right, so connected that we think it is something that we have accomplished. Rather, it is our allowing God to touch our lives and His goodness to absorb into our beings.

We should ask ourselves, "Are we having more of these times, or less, and why?" Either answer to the question calls us to allow more of this bliss and partnership with God to occur. Most often, it is our distraction with our selfish motives which are easily learned from the behavior of our society that prevents this.

Search your memory for the times when you were in the groove, cherish them, and plan on having many more. This will happen if we focus daily on allowing the awareness of God's magnificent creation to keep us in our groove.

## What Are You After in the Hereafter?

When you ponder this question, mostly pleasurable words come to mind: joy, peace, understanding, happiness, contentment, no more pain, no more worry, are just a few that would be given in response. When you stop to think, these are all human descriptions of what we hope for.

Refer to the line in the "Our Father" that says, "Thy will be done on Earth as it is in heaven." What our Father has prepared for us, it is said, "Eye has not seen nor ear has heard what God has in store for us." That tells me our imagination is worthless when it comes to the hereafter.

When I go back, the things we are humanly after are actually things we were born with, and somehow let slip away through some of life's experiences. To have these back we must connect with God and allow His will to be done. God works with us, through us, and for us. And when we are perfectly aligned with God in those moments in life that are realized, we get a sample of what is in the hereafter. So, I ask you to turn away from selfish wishes and dreams for the hereafter, and turn to trusting in God's will, thereby connecting with what we should be after.

## Choices

Oh, what freedom and free will "choices" provide us with. Isn't it great to be able to decide our fates and destinies? Well, I am not so sure it is all that wonderful. Being able to choose presents us with tremendous responsibility that forms our conscience and character. The other chore or task is the numerous choices one makes every day.

What time do I get up in the morning, what do I wear, what shall I have for breakfast, and it goes on all day.

Now, when we make choices, what is the motive of our choices? Is it for the most gain, most pleasure, or most comfort? Or, is it for doing the most good for the most people that day? Well, if the answer is the second choice, you also attain your first motive because your pleasure and comfort and peace come to you from doing good for other people. But if you take the first motive as first choice, you will never be fulfilled or satisfied.

The best answer to any choice is found inside of us, because that is where God resides if we allow Him to. When we trust in God's wisdom and all-knowing, we can be assured of a good outcome or result. When we leave everything to our human selves to decide, much doubt, anxiety, and second guessing appears and makes our lives difficult and stressful. So, by allowing God to come into our lives in all things, choices become very easy and confident. Therefore, first and foremost, the most important and valuable choice we can make is to allow God to live in our hearts and lives.

## Easter Morn

Christ is risen now and forever
To show us where we are all in this together.
A human life given to learn and grow
That our spiritual life is eternal you know.
Death was defeated when Easter occurred.
Now it is nothing more than a word.
Jesus is our teacher, our model, our hero
So listen and learn and your risk is zero.
Jesus certainly showed us the way.
Let us think about it each and every day.
And as we do, we will be peaceful and strong
All because of the lesson of "Easter Morn."

## Legacy

Legacy is a much used word in today's vocabulary. It means inheritance and what you are leaving for your family and community.

Many people hurry and scurry to obtain as much wealth and accomplishments as possible while they are able to. And many feel very satisfied and comfortable with this achievement.

Now this collection of material and possessions will last until they are either forgotten or squandered away. These things lose meaning as time goes by. May I suggest an alternative legacy of knowledge and example to be passed on with each generation?

The knowledge of why we are here in this world and the example of how to use this in a loving and unselfish manner has substance that is everlasting. The legacy of Jesus Christ is still being recognized and enjoyed by all who care to, even after 2,000 years. This legacy will last forever, whereas material things have eroded and decayed and been forgotten. Each of us humans can be a witness to Jesus' legacy, the word of truth, and the light of love that will burn eternally.

One legacy will be a faded memory, while the other becomes a way of life.

## This Is Beautiful

Beauty is a word and a sense that most of our society is infatuated with. Movie stars, models, athletes, are all looked upon as beautiful. The admired list goes on to flowers, jewelry, clothes, and houses. The reality of the subject is, all of God's creation is beautiful, even the rocks and the deserts.

We humans often fail to recognize and appreciate this entire gift of beauty. There is also beauty in things we cannot see, but can sense and feel and know that they are there. Beauty never fails to expose itself to us, we just fail to recognize and want to experience it. This can change when we invite into our soul the everlasting existence each creature and object has in everything that surrounds us. The laugh of a child, the radiance of a bride, the contentment of the father, and the joyful tears of the mother are but a few of the descriptions of what I'm talking about. The smell of fresh mown hay, hearing the umpire yell, "Play ball," the soft skin of a baby, and yes, even the cry of a baby are all beautiful things to me.

The beauty of beauty is that it is free for our enjoyment. There is no fee or gimmick, no need for imagination, just simply look for it.

## Missing the Point

Many of our religious services are filled with an excess of glory, worship, and adoration. Jesus came into the world to show us He was one of us, the human creation we all share.

We know from our social circles, we are most comfortable with people of our own beliefs and characteristics. He came to us to be one of us, and not to seek glory and adoration. He came to teach and seek love.

Yet in many of our prayers and hymns we continue to exhort praise, glorification, thanksgiving, and requests. Even in the liturgy of our Catholic Mass, I don't see anywhere that we tell Jesus, Who is present at the Eucharist, that we love Him.

I don't believe there is a better way to show and express love for someone than to sincerely tell them in actions and words. My first grade teacher taught me a little prayer that could be used at Mass or anytime in life. "Jesus, I believe in You, I hope in You, I love You with all my heart." I feel this is very appropriate for a relationship with Jesus Christ.

To love and be loved is all that He asks.

## Spirit

First we are there, then we are here.
Time to get the search into high gear.
The know of who and why
Will result in how high
Our awareness and happiness will be
In the next phase of eternity.
Life is so interesting with our spirit.
If only we would allow ourselves to hear it.
So as days fly by in a hurry
And we all run around in a flurry
Be patient to hear the sound and see the light
That awaits us with tremendous might.
We will return to the shore as before
To be with the One we all adore.

## GPS

Many travelers who drive to a new destination use this device for accurate directions. I believe it stands for Global Positioning System. It is of great service to the large number of people who either own or borrow this tool.

Now when it comes to directions in our moral and spiritual life, we have GPS and more in Jesus Christ and the life and the way He has shown us. The many accounts and stories of His time on Earth with us show which turns to take on our path through life. Also, if we take a wrong turn, He instructs us on how to correct our direction.

Now this device for guidance is only helpful if one has a destination or goal he or she is intent on reaching. Many of our lives are lived in a lateral or parallel motion. This could be because we have fear of or just aren't ready to advance to the fullness of life that Jesus offers us. When you have total confidence in your teacher and guide, the fear you may have will vanish or disappear forever.

## Relationships

Everything in our lives revolves around relationships. There are many descriptive words that can be used on this subject. Close or distant, meaningful or polite, satisfying or frustrating, solid or shaky, cooperative or competitive, loving or selfish, are some of these words that are worth thinking about. All these comparisons show one side of substance, truth and caring; and another of symbolism, pretense, and apathy. How we live these relationships with the people around us and how we live our relationship with God is surely worth looking at and studying. We very possibly would be surprised if we took the time and effort to do this. We also could discover how we relate to ourselves.

*Identification.* First of all, let us identify where we are. To do this successfully, we must be quite honest and open within ourselves. To be deceptive and foolish would be wasting our time and effort and most certainly give an answer that lies within one side of the descriptive words above.

So, let us explore how we relate to others and why. By asking why, I mean to examine the attitude and motives we have in relationships. Of course, the primary and most important relationship is with God. When there is one of substance, truth, and love, all the other relationships will follow this path and be rewarding and fulfilling. After examining how we relate to others and why, we need to decide where we are and where we would like to be in our relationships.

Now that we have a goal, the next step is to express our desires with actions. Ingredients such as respect, trust, communication, honesty, compassion, forgiveness, cooperation, and compromise lead to healthy, loving and growing relationships. When we use these basics as a foundation, we will have a correct attitude and motive.

A good, strong relationship requires that we give to each other as well as practice self-sacrifice at times for the sake of the other. This fulfills the old saying, "It is in giving that we receive." How we relate to God is answered in how we treat and relate to our families and neighbors who surround us in life. It is in this expression that God sees our innermost thoughts and feelings. He does not see what we tell Him or tell ourselves.

Let us all reach God through the people around us and good relationships with them.

### Christmas Eternal

Bethlehem was the scene.
The fulfillment of our dream.
Jesus came physically to be with us.
Taught us how to live amid all this human fuss.
He will come to us daily if we let Him in.
We will be our own Bethlehem.
This place I refer to is our heart.
Hold Him close and never let Him depart.
His truth and love is all we need
For our spiritual life to be filled and succeed.
As He and we share this gift with everyone
This great Christmas joy who is God's only Son.

## Getting to Know You

Did you ever stop and think how many people really know you, and you know them? Surprised, aren't you? I am fortunate to know several, which is more than most people. Oh, of course, we have been introduced to many people in our lifetimes, and have even lived with some in the same household comfortably for years and years. But really, how many of them actually know us? How many have we allowed to know us? How many have accepted the invitation, if given?

When we stay protected and keep innermost feelings as secrets, we feel secure. However, unless we give totally of ourselves, how can anyone totally know us? The greatest example of this is God offering His Son Jesus Christ to all of us to get to know Him. If we keep something, anything, between us and Him, we will never know Him. Powerful, isn't it, and yet so very true.

Even Jesus' disciples may not have known Him. We all heard of Peter denying Him three times. "I do not know this man." I believe he was telling the truth.

I feel I must repeat my words. "Unless we give totally of ourselves, how can anyone totally know us?" Jesus gave us the invitation to know Him, His greatest gift. Yet, here we are in the year 2012 A.D. and so many have returned a "no" to His invitation. What are we afraid of? Is it being close to someone who actually knows us?

Well, when we get to know Him, we actually will get to know ourselves, from whence we came. It is beautiful, and yet, so many have refused and said "no."

Another side effect is, when we know Him, we also know everyone else. Scary, isn't it? But, oh so true. The invitation continues and another decision comes our way.

Would you care to now and forever get to know you?

## Imagination

When our children were young, I discouraged the belief in Santa Claus, Easter Bunny, Tooth Fairy, and all the imaginary figures of American society, like Mickey Mouse, the Disney Club, and Looney Tunes. I heard plenty of criticism of this from other parents for spoiling children's fun. I believe it sends them the wrong message about make-believe, and where it starts, and where it ends. I fear when they grow older, and search for God and spirituality, confusion is possible, because of the familiarity of pretend in their lives.

God is very real, but not in the sense of a physical figure or vision. But, this is the concept of God most humans have. God is a spirit, and can be spiritually felt rather than physically seen. God's spirit resides in our spirit if we allow Him in, and not in our physical bodies, the bodies all other humans see.

So, let us look to and for the spirit being in others, and hopefully feel God's presence there also.

The human body is a mask and image-maker to other humans, and is used as our spirit sees the need to. This happens when people's egos direct their bodies to do something wrong or harmful. Remember the comedian's line, "The devil made me do it"?

This also happens when people who have God residing in their spirits do something good or helpful. So, let us reject the phony images of human make-believe and embrace the reality of spiritual life.

Why do so many people cling to the make believe so strongly and so loyally? It could be because when they are busy pretending, they don't have to face their own spirituality. Who am I, and how can my relationship with God become closer? We don't like to ask oftentimes until we are of old age and nearing the end of our human lives. An example of this is all the fiction books and movies that people turn to. Also, the popularity of soap operas and amusement parks support this observation. So, I encourage everyone to stop getting away, but instead get with "who" we are.

## The Good Book

Oh what glory
Just to tell a story.
Must be interesting to read
The account of word and deed.
It is all contained in a big book.
Take the time and take a look.
The teaching and the healing
Is all very appealing.
In it is all we need to know
Before it is time for us to go.
I'm sure you know the title.
Of course, it is the Holy Bible.

## Will Power

I have always been in awe of the power of the will. I know I've done things in my life I didn't think I could, and all because of will power.

My mother always commented "If there is a will, there is a way." So, not only does the will have power, it also has thought and ingenuity.

This leads me to the words in the Our Father, "Thy kingdom come, Thy will be done, on Earth, as it is in heaven." This tells me that there is such a thing as God's Will.

A priest reflecting on his lifetime, said his obedience to his superiors was against his will, but came to realize that God was directing those changes in his life. He commented that the score was God- 4, Father -0. Each time, God's will gave him opportunities and lessons he would not have had otherwise.

We don't always have superiors or authority to obey, but have free will to choose. This is why when you say the Our Father, think of the words you say about, "Thy will be done" and try to search and allow God's Will to be made aware to you. It will be, and hopefully we can use our free will to choose God's Will. If that happens, we all succeed in finding our way.

## Trust and Loyalty

We all place our trust in certain people during our lives, and when we trust, we tend to be loyal to that person. Those around us like spouses, parents, children, teachers, pastors, and hopefully employers, usually deserve our trust because they are loyal to us. This is sometimes referred to as the "circle of trust."

We all have had our trust betrayed at some time in our lives, and we can recall the pain and hurt and the insult we felt. All of us who are in a circle of trust deserve to receive trust and loyalty, as well as having the responsibility to give it. This is a big part of our character and our ability to have good, lasting relationships. We earn people's trust and respect by our example and our actions.

Of course, sometimes we humans do fail in this regard. But, When we trust in God, we have an eternal guarantee of His trust without fail. No doubts needed. So, I continue to search for God's Will and generosity in my life knowing my trust in God will never be betrayed or failed.

Let us all strive to be loyal and thankful to God.

## Joy

A balmy, sunny day.
The grass is green. It is May.
My name is Joy.
A wholesome person wearing a smile.
One who is aware, not in denial.
My name is Joy.
A baby's skin so soft to my touch.
A child who is free, doesn't ask for much.
My name is Joy.
A delicious meal prepared with love.
Our senses filled, with the eating of.
My name is Joy.
Helping another when they are in need.
The reward received from this good deed.
My name is Joy.
A bride and groom being united.
Their vows exchanged and recited.
My name is Joy.
Living each moment in the Spirit.
Allow God to come in and experience It.
My name is Joy.

## Awaken

When I was a young child, I heard a comment from my mother about someone who had passed away. She said, "He died in his sleep, he went to sleep and never woke up." How many of us have gone to sleep and haven't woken up at present?

Have we gone to sleep by the lullaby of early religious teaching, and the training and distraction of society and its behavior? Quotes such as, "I am the Way, the Truth, and the Light" and "The light shined in the darkness, and the darkness grasped it not," are reminders. Let us awaken to the light of God through Jesus and His teachings. Search through scriptures to find instructions on where to find God, our Creator. If you are aware, they will stand out in a bright light to show you the answer. So, I challenge you to search for God within you, where He is present, instead of without, where He is only imagined by your human mind.

Awakening to a new dawn of spirituality will illuminate all of life's opportunities, and also allowing God within us to be a partner in our eternal life.

## Heaven

Pope John Paul teaches us heaven is not a place to go, but rather a state of being, a place where our spirit and soul exist. The lyrics from a song say, "Everybody wants to go to heaven, but nobody wants to go now."

I do believe we can go there while living life here on Earth, but very, very few ever will. It takes a full communion with God and we take this lifetime to learn the feeling of totality that connects us. It is our journey to home.

If we yearn for and search for our real heavenly home, we will reach it much sooner. Since our measure of time is irrelevant, our eternal realization is the sooner or later I refer to.

So, are you searching for this heavenly state of being, or are you looking for a place in the sky or outer space, where your individual imagination is fulfilled? Do you want to postpone your rendezvous with God by clinging to a fantasy of convenience, or would you rather connect the real you with the Real God Our Creator?

### Eternity's Answer

When one ponders eternity
Many encounter uncertainty.
How can this be? There is no such thing.
There must be an end, if there's a beginning.
The fact that eternity always did exist
Is the essence and beauty of all this.
The measure of always is forever.
The substance of this is very clever.
So, in the cloud of our human state
To understand and accept is our eventual fate.
This is one of the many things we cannot control.
Unless we allow it to enter our eternal soul.

## Easter—"The Glorious Lesson"

What does the glorious resurrection of Christ Jesus teach us, and what have we learned from it? Life is eternal.

We learned that when our human existence ends, life continues, as Jesus' human life taught us.

After this great event, we now know the real meaning and description of all our lives. They are everlasting and of much more substance and value than mere human existence and deeds. As the resurrection defeated death and rendered it meaningless, we are all freed from the fear humanity projects to us daily.

The central lesson is Jesus didn't only die for us, He rose with us all. Death is temporary, where life is forever. So, let us focus on the lesson taught to us each Easter, and not glorify the beautiful story we hear each season. Let us give thanks for the gift of the lesson, and not for the drama of the event.

## Taste and See

"Taste and see the goodness of the Lord" are words from a hymn sung in our church. The goodness of the Lord is all around us, in many forms and life situations. The key word here is taste. Unless we partake of some of this goodness, we may never see it in all of its beauty.

You may say, "Yes, there is goodness in the world, but also there is a lot of evil." This is true, but the evil is from man and its ego at work.

The wrong choices we make create the evil we see and it definitely does not come from God. These wrong choices are made because of the lack of God's presence in our lives at that time. The world governments want to remove God from our lives in order to control us more completely. Others choose to use the false image of God to commit murder and kill millions in His name. Now more than ever, we need to taste and see the goodness of the Lord.

So, come to the table of goodness God has prepared, and taste, eat, digest, and embrace the love that is in every encounter. There is no better way to sustain our life, now and forever.

## Health

Did you ever notice how concerned people are about their physical health, while paying little attention to their spiritual health? We are constantly seeking medical treatment and advice for various ailments and illnesses. Another factor of high awareness these days is nutrition and proper balance of good intakes.

This reminds me of the observation of some doctors that there is no such thing as illness or disease; rather, there is a lack or void of good health. It seems the negative approach is the one most often taken.

So, I challenge you to examine your spiritual condition and the ways you are nourishing it. Are you practicing the positive virtues of love, kindness, compassion, generosity, forgiveness, and understanding? Are you allowing God to dwell in your life, and continuing to search deeper still in order to become even closer to Him than you presently are?

Good spiritual health also leads to better physical health as well. Which one of the two is your priority today and tomorrow?

## A Friend

Right now I need a friend.
One that is strong, will not bend.
Maybe the bottle will understand.
Short term, yes, long term, bad end.
So where do I turn for friendship and feeling?
Someone who is warm and full of healing.
A creature with ability to fill a hole.
It may or may not have a soul.
Because God's creation can reach us all
With things and creatures both large and small.
Let me look for the touch or the grace.
Just being and waiting for an embrace.
Friends are there, we must search and find.
They are waiting also, the most celestial kind.
Could be that my friend is lonely too.
And possibly it ends up being you.

## You Reap What You Sow

Relationship is an often used word with little thought given to the substance of it. It is often used because we relate to everybody and everything we come into contact with over our entire lifetime.

I think the old saying, "You reap what you sow," is very applicable in describing relationships. Not only is the sowing or beginning important, but also how we nurture and grow and intensify it as we live our lives.

Relationships are powerful as they can be fulfilling and joyous, but can also be destructive and painful. Far too many times we fail to admit the latter and do whatever it takes to end them.

In the good relationships, we tend to take them for granted, and never reap or enjoy the magnitude of the potential that, I might add, is unlimited. This is certainly true with our relationship with God.

Every time we recognize that everyone and everything is a gift from God, then God is relating to us in a living way. You might ask, how can a bad or harmful relationship be a gift from God? I ask you to ponder about this as possibly a moment for you to learn about choices. Of course, "choices" could lead to a whole other subject to discuss later.

## Complete Love

Many years ago, my youngest son, Tony, was riding with me in our truck. His age was early elementary school. I don't recall how the conversation started, but Tony proclaimed a profound truth in the form of a question. "Dad, don't you know you cannot love anyone, unless you love everybody?"

As the years go by, more and more, I realize how accurate this is. We are all part of God's Creation; therefore, we can't love God completely if we don't love all of His Creation. This is very simple and basic, and yet, a child speaks of this so clearly.

I understand to many this is a huge challenge, but until this comes about, any love we have for others is incomplete or not whole.

After pondering this awareness, let us be conscious of it each and every day as we relate to others we come into contact with. After all, this tells us that they are part of us, and we are part of them as creatures of God. If we do this, we will feel the results in a huge, total way. Our definition and quality of love will be genuine and complete.

## How Do You Spell Relief?

Please God, take the pain away.
Even if only for a day.
So I can use my memory of how it was, and how it will be.
For I'm sure we were meant to be pain free.
Pain is like a war of attrition
So it behooves us to stay in good condition.
If pain is less, we are less contrary
Because we know it is only temporary.
So, dear Lord, chase it away
Till I reunite with you on that day.
To be home again will be great. Hey. Hey!

## Life

Many times we hear speakers and preachers encourage us to "change our lives." I believe it is much more important to "find our life" than to change it.

Let us search and find "who" we are. This is the foundation for changing anything about the way we live. We seem so concerned about the what, the where, the when, and the why about life, we don't start at the beginning with the "who."

The "who" is the spirit created in the image and likeness of God, by God, out of total love. We all start here, and remain here, if we stay with God in our human endeavor.

Our humanity is formed by our surroundings and our learned behavior, and is tempted by our ego. This often becomes a negative to our spiritual connection. It also can be an opportunity to learn and grow and ultimately fuse with our Creator and His love.

So, look for the opportunity, and follow its path, and discard the negative aspect of your false human perception and ego. Finding your life is euphoric and fulfilling.

## Before Abraham Became

The "I Am" meaning is that God is, always was, and always will be. This is the eternal spirit that we refer to as God. Jesus is part of God, always. We talk about Advent as the period of waiting for Jesus to come. This is reversed. Jesus is the One who is waiting for each one of us. He is there always, and invites us to come to Him from where we came. God waits for us to come home.

## Wake Me Up

Lord, I am so weary
As there are many people dreary.
Show me the spark to ignite once more
To get myself up off the floor.
There is still so much good I want to do
And yet, I feel like a worn out shoe.
A push or shove in the right direction
Would give this situation some correction.
As I sit here pondering and wait
Anxious to leave the starting gate.
So I may do wondrous things with my time
Until the day I cross the finish line.

## Finding God

I just watched a news program that was describing the last moments of Steve Jobs's life. His eulogy was given by his sister, and she quoted his last words as, "Oh Wow, Oh Wow, Oh Wow." The news commentators were discussing whether, or if, Steve found God.

I believe that concept is reversed. God finds us, even though many hide from or deny Him. God is always here and always there. He will forever come to you and be by you whenever you choose to recognize His presence.

So, the word "finding" could be replaced by "discovering." We don't need to wait until our last words to discover Who is there, and the love and empowerment that comes with Him. We don't need an appointment to allow God into our hearts, minds, and souls. Just open the door.

It is possible that is what Steve Jobs did.

## May Sunrise

As the sun rises over the hill
And everything is perfectly still.
A kaleidoscope of colors appear
As the rays reflect the atmosphere.
It is time to absorb and digest
The beauty of nature and all of the rest.
So much is there for us to capture.
A painting of such produces rapture.
There is nothing more pristine
Than the moment of the picturesque scene.
So take time to look and enjoy.
And don't be humanly coy.
For this part of spiritual heaven
Will be ours to feel forever.

## To All Christians

As we all pray for things in our lives, let us ask ourselves how our thoughts are directed, and how our feelings are expressed. Do we pray for our wishes, wants, and benefits for ourselves, or do we pray for God's will and also consider the effect on others? Which did Jesus Christ show and instruct us to do?

When Jesus prayed in the garden before His crucifixion, He asked His Father to take the suffering away from Him and then said, "Not my will, but yours be done." Jesus knew this great sacrifice was God's will, and that it should be done, not for His benefit, but for the benefit of every other soul.

The Our Father says, "Thy will be done on Earth as it is in heaven." How do we say this prayer? Do we mean what we say, or do we ask God to give us what we think we need and make us feel good? Perhaps we forget to sacrifice, if it is God's will for the benefit of others. Do we ask for better health, successful business, beautiful possessions, things that only benefit ourselves? Consider the contrast and see why many of the gifts we pray for are not influenced by God. One is a prayer for love, and the good of the whole Christian community, the other is a prayer of selfishness and short personal gain.

Prayer is about a relationship, not a contract or deal. This relationship needs to be established in order for communication to begin. This same requirement is true in everyday life, with our families and friends, the whole Body of Christ, which is our fellow brother or sister. Therefore, prayer is something to be lived every day, in all events, during our lives. The repetition of words does not make prayer more effective. It instead demonstrates a lack of faith that we are being heard. Prayer in the relationship and spirit of love will be listened to by our God. Prayer in the spirit of self, may not be heard, much less answered. If we are one with God, we belong to everyone, not one self. To be One with God, it is necessary to know love.

Love is the key that opens the door to all things. When it is present, good things happen in our lives, and in the lives of those around us. When love is absent, people search for material possessions, self-gratification, and power to make themselves happy. Needless to say, the search will be never ending, and their goals unattainable. Love must be lived and not spoken. Acts of love are spontaneous, unscheduled. They are expressed even though not required. Acts of love truly are unconditional. If conditions or personal gain are present, love is only a spoken word. Many people say, "I love you" and yet their actions totally contradict what they have said. Love is an expression of kindness, caring, compassion, forgiveness, and togetherness. It is not a word used to obtain from others what we ourselves wish or desire.

Consider the contrast here: "What is love in our lives? When we glance at the way we live, what do we see?" If love is present, we see everything; or, do we see nothing because love is absent?

With all of my love and the everlasting love of Christ . . .

# Conclusion

At the end of most plays and books, this word "Conclusion" describes the last chapter or scene. If we look at our human life journey, we all have a conclusion to it as well. How will our conclusion be viewed and received by those whose lives we have touched?

That depends on the results of our efforts and search for God our Creator. If we have reached a high level of discovery and awareness, it will be manifested in the love we have for each other as well as for God who dwells there. We are the author of our last chapter and summary.

What we do in the present will have a profound effect on the outcome. Each day we write another paragraph. Will we tie or connect all of our life's experiences and lessons into a meaningful transformation to our next residence? Hopefully we will be one with our all-loving God and all of His happiness for eternity.

## A Child's Song

Please God, open the eyes to my heart so I can see you. When I heard this, I felt, "What a beautiful prayer for each and every one of us." I don't need to write anything more in this paragraph.

## The Light

"The light shineth in the darkness and the darkness grasped it not." These words taken from sacred scripture have a tremendous impact on me, and of course, on all humanity.

Jesus Christ came as the light to all the world. Many people have accepted Jesus Christ as their Lord and Savior, and believed they are saved because of this belief of faith. But have they accepted His teachings and example that are the "light of the world"? Are we allowing the light to shine and manifest itself in our lives? If we don't, we are the darkness grasping it not.

Jesus said, "I am the Way, the Truth and the Light." These are the substantial gifts that God gave to us through His Son. The love that Jesus spoke to us about is the love of God which is total and for all. How complete we choose to love in life is how bright this light in our lives will be allowed to shine.

So let us strive to love in the manner Jesus showed and taught us. Believing that faith in Jesus is our membership card for salvation is not the message Jesus came to teach us. Rather, "Love one another as I have loved you" and you will be grasping the Light.

## Love Motive

When and if we choose to love another, it is good to examine our motives. Some of these are: it feels really good (warm and fuzzy) to love someone; it brings a return from another to us (also feels good); it solves (fulfills) a requirement for our personal salvation. These are all very popular and evident with a large part of our human family. These also point to a selfish component. When we give our total unselfish love to God from whom all love exists, our self becomes unimportant to us.

Now, through God's Will, we can become distributors of this eternal love. It all becomes a beautiful circle when we live in this spirit. Blessings and joy will be plentiful when we choose to serve God by loving all others. But look to the top shelf and the high road for these rewards, because they won't be in the material form or secular values.

You might say this all sounds good, but how do I start? I say to start this very moment with the people closest around you, and your community, and it will accelerate each day, and grow to include each life you touch during yours.

## What Is Spirit?

Spirit is life: a gift from God.
Spirit is our inner soul.
Spirit is our ability to love.
Spirit is our attitude.
Spirit is our relationship and connection to God.
Spirit is our joy.
Spirit is our understanding of truth.
Spirit is eternal.
Spirit is our gratitude.
Spirit is our compassion.
Spirit is our gentleness.
Spirit is our warmth.
Spirit is our strength.
Spirit is our courage.
Spirit is who we are.

## Enlightenment

My wife came home from the hairdresser and was elated. After 40 years of styling her hair, she was taught about the natural beauty and condition of her beautiful hair. She learned how to not use all the shampoos and creams that dry hair out and straighten it unnaturally. She was working against the beauty and health of nature's gift of hair. I told her how happy I was with her newfound knowledge, and said this could apply to hers and everybody's lives in every area.

To learn about nutrition and physical exercise and all the metabolic systems of our bodies is also most beneficial and enlightening.

The next step is to explore the nature of our spiritual life. Let us become aware of our spiritual existence and how well we understand it and how well we seek growth and connection with our loving Creator who is God. Think of how happy we can be in this lifetime when we see the light and truth of God's love and manifestation. To use the quote of a Sufi poet on God's invitation to us: "Come dance with Me."

## Morality

Most people think of morality as the distinction between right and wrong. I believe it has a much broader meaning.

It isn't always only the choice of right or wrong, but also the attitude and degree of reaction we use toward a given situation. Contrasts of these are: pro-active or passive, engaged from within or controlled by the outside, or looking for a compromise when you are undecided. Metaphoric examples are: on the fence, a foot on each path, covering your behind. We are pulled each way sometimes for many reasons, such as family influence, traditional behavior, being politically correct, ethical, social justice, and other terms that come into play. Now we are back to being indifferent, afraid of rejection, and being timid to ask ourselves for sacrifice when required.

I aspire and hope (or pray) for the wisdom, strength, and the courage to arrive at a thoughtful, but more importantly, a loving decision from my heart and soul, and the passion to carry it out in an outward and convincing way.

I challenge all of you to make morality a daily way of life in an open manner and not a hidden or silent one.

# 2 | Want Life to be Nice? Here's Some Advice

## Forgiveness

The most important task to becoming peaceful and happy is to learn forgiveness. Unless we learn to forgive others and ourselves, we will retain feelings of anger, bitterness, and hatred. These emotional feelings lead to physical symptoms and health problems. When we don't forgive others, we are unable to forgive ourselves when we hurt someone. The place to start is to ask for forgiveness from others. If this is granted, we can begin to forgive ourselves. Sometimes this part is more difficult than forgiving others.

I will give you one example of being asked. Our parish priest wrongly used some of the parish funds for personal use. When this was discovered, Father spoke to the parish at each Mass, and admitted his mistake, and sincerely asked all of us to forgive him. As we exited the church, Father stood by the door. One by one passed by without a word, and many looked down instead of at him. I, myself, stopped, looked Father in the eyes, shook his hand, and said, "Father, I forgive you," and then moved on. I'm sure a few others may have done the same thing, but I believe it was a small minority. Both Father and I were freed from all the negative emotions mentioned earlier.

Another example is the sexual conduct scandal that was widespread in the Catholic Church. When this came to light, the victims came forward demanding monetary compensation. Large sums of money were paid to these people by the dioceses as settlement. All the press accounts of these events were sensationalized about the exact amounts each one received. Nowhere in these reports was there a mention of forgiveness by all. Many of these victims were suffering from emotional and physical ailments.

I submit to you that the money will not relieve the pain and misery for them, but that sincere forgiveness by all involved will heal them dramatically. The usual reply is, "I can never be repaired or repaid enough for my suffering." Aha, if only they would forgive, the healing and joy would be back in their lives.

I know it doesn't happen quickly, but it is the beginning of the path to a happy ending. When we forgive, another door is opened, and an obstacle removed from being in harmony with God

A real roadblock to forgiveness is when the abuser keeps on hurting the other person. How do you forgive if the injustice and pain continue to occur? I don't have an answer to that. The closest I can come to an answer is to live in a forgiving spirit and persevere and outlast the wrong. There isn't even a hint of easy in this area.

## What Are You Going to Do About It?

So many issues in life are important and controversial. These are times to think, reason, feel, and study them. After all these steps are taken, you will have come to a belief, and a decision.

Now most people feel secure in their effort and convey their thoughts to whoever will listen. This is good but very anemic in solving these issues. Rhetoric is the path of choice and often told and repeated to the same people.

The crying need at this point is action. Set the example by doing, and also start the networking process. We all know someone somewhere who can make a difference with their position and credibility. Get the snowball rolling. Be a player and not a spectator. Remember, there is strength in numbers. Be active, and create good results as you go forward.

When you see people benefit, it is a good feeling and, I might add, is contagious. It usually leads to more. The question of the present to those who understand: "Okay, now, what are you going to do about it?"

## The Computer Is Down

The computer age is here to stay.
Where else could you shop on ebay?
Information comes on we don't really need.
But, oh boy, it comes in at high speed.
Then some days it lets us down.
They say a virus or worm is in town.
We could go back to as before
And go shopping at the store.
Turn on the radio and TV
For the news to hear and see.
Become more active, get off your butt.
Don't be a prisoner to the technology rut.
I say, hold up, we don't need the fix.
I can live without it at age sixty-six.

## The Leaning Fence

A visitor from another country came to a farm in Iowa. A nearby fence was leaning to a great degree. She commented that, before she left, the fence needed to be straightened. Of course, this was delayed to the last day before it was addressed, and made upright and strong once again.

This story is similar to many of our personal lives in that most of us have leaning fences that need to be righted. And likewise, many of us push them off until the last minute or day. There is a risk in waiting, for that last day opportunity may have vanished for some unexpected reason.

So, it is wise to take a look and inspect our personal fences, and our spiritual attitude, and to start to straighten and mend them where needed immediately. We will feel much better and relieved to have our character standing tall and erect once again. To delay is an invitation to weakness and indecision to control our lives. Sometimes, it takes a visitor or stranger to wake us up.

## The Three Cs

Jealousy is a very troubling feeling, as it is a conflict within us. It is understood as wanting or craving what someone else has. To pursue what and who jealousy directs us to is harmful and painful. Jealousy usually begins with what I call the three Cs: Comparison, Competition, Catastrophe.

Initially, we are *Comparing* ourselves or possessions to those of another person. Secondly, we begin to *Compete* for whatever our desire is, such as money, house, car, or any other material objects. Also, humans tend to *Compete* for the attention and emotional happiness of another. This usually happens with siblings, friends, or even parents. When living this path, hatred and bitterness often surface, as well as unkind and cruel behavior such as lying, deceit, and manipulation. The result of all the above is *Catastrophe*. Sooner or later, we realize it is a cancer in our character and happiness, and hopefully let go of it, and heal once more.

So, let us not begin the comparison and competition and rather leave that for sporting events. Also, recall two of the Ten Commandments: Thou shalt not covet thy neighbor's goods. Thou shalt not covet thy neighbor's wife. If you have jealousy now, dispose of it, forever.

Another comment often heard is, "It just isn't fair." Well, I like to answer, "The fair is in August." Fairness has little to do with life. It isn't the other person you see as you do. But rather, it is all about you. It is up to us to be grateful for what we have, and to realize that it is *enough* for our well-being and happiness. When we accept it as enough, rewards will appear in abundance—rewards that you didn't realize existed.

So, why not accept the challenge to visit the flip-side of jealousy, and find contentment and joy for yourself, and those around you?

## Dawn

A new day is dawning.
Time to arise and stop yawning.
Another opportunity of life lies ahead
Surely for hope and not to dread.
I ask what to do with this day.
The farmer says, "When the sun shines, make hay."
This metaphor can be used in any situation.
Helps us to avoid prolonged deliberation.
Many others help us to know.
Such as, "Go with the flow" and "Reap what you sow."
Let us do well with this wonderful chance
In a positive way, all of life to enhance.

## Yes or No

Many things happen in life to us and for us that are impossible to explain. Some things are for the better or good, and some are the opposite.

Now, we often say, "That incident or situation was out of our control." This may be true, but whether we choose to accept it or refuse it is up to us. So we do have control over our lives when we decide to say "Yes or No" to all things offered to us, constantly.

Of course, we don't like a painful event, but if we accept it and move on, healing takes place. If we say "no", the pain and suffering continue to torment us.

The same is true of a happy or joyous opportunity. We could say "no" because of fear or skepticism, or because we have a low self-image and say, "I really don't deserve this." Saying "yes" also carries a responsibility and commitment that many of us are unwilling to make long term.

So, we should always look at the large picture when we choose our answers to everyday life. Which one will bring peace, joy, contentment, self-worth, and healing, and are we brave enough to choose it? This is our constant challenge to exercise our free-will which does produce outcomes. Choose to not go through life attributing every good or bad thing that happens to either God or the devil. We do possess that powerful choice to answer "Yes" or "No."

## Adventure

The other day, I delivered a Holstein bull to another farm, which I had never been to. It was interesting and thought provoking.

My first stop was to have the animal tested at the vet clinic. This went well, except for one situation where the bull made a wrong turn, and damaged some of their equipment. The reaction by one person there was that of a habit that I've experienced in this area all of my life. Something gets broken, and a string of cuss words and expressed anger come flying out. When will we grow past this?

Next, being inexperienced driving, I made a wrong turn which caused me distress. Panic always shows up at such a time. When will I grow past this? Back on track, and heading in an area I had never gone before, I saw a new and interesting sight, but it seemed like a long way. As I got closer, the road kept narrowing and was very hilly. Once again, fear and anxiety show up, as to where is it taking me. When will I grow past this? The trip ended well when I arrived at my destination, and my return was uneventful, although the road back seemed much shorter, when it was familiar. I need more trust.

The comparison to life itself is: a wrong turn can be corrected. Trust and confidence will erase the fear, anxiety, and panic, and allow me to break the foolish habit I exhibited.

## Doubting

What is it about doubt
That makes us pout?
The indecision, the fear, the unknown.
These are things that make life seem like a loan.
Rather, it is not borrowed, but given.
Ours to do with, for the living.
So, why have doubts when you can be sure
Everything is worthwhile when motive is pure.
Free yourself from the doubt and the waste
And life will have a much better taste.
To believe in oneself is necessary.
For this you become an accuracy
Not of numbers and percentages and such.
But of what is real and what is out of touch.
Get rid of doubt and all of its friends.
You will be confident in the beginning as well as the end.

## The Unexpected

Do you ever notice how many times something very unexpected happens to us? Is this just luck or coincidence? I think not.

The surprises happen when we have an unrealistic or imaginary view of the future. We want certain things to go the way we wish them. Now, if that wish is a real possibility, hopefully it will be fulfilled and satisfied. Of course, the opposite side is that your wish is often impossible. It just "ain't gonna happen." If we can separate the real from the imagined, we will naturally have few unexpected events in our life.

For this, we need to let go of the "way things have always been" in the past, of course coupled with expectations built upon reason, logic, and understanding of our created nature. When we cooperate with our created intention, many good things occur. When we are foolhardy, and in denial of the truth, our stubbornness becomes pathological.

How often do we say, "I should have known better"? This leads to multiple frustrations and disappointments, becoming very routine. Some say they are "down on their luck." Even though we arrange our expectations to our advantage, there will be rare misses in what we expect, because perfection is not a human trait.

Remember, sometimes something we don't expect turns out to be extremely beneficial and good. Let us strive for a positive balance in what we look forward to in our life's "Expectations."

## Honesty

Why be cute when no need to be?
Why be coy, trying to spread glee?
Many play act and pretend
Believing it leads to an advantaged end.
When dealing with people
Be as straight as a church steeple.
Always better to be honest and real
As you look for a fair deal.
No other compliment goes as high
As someone says you are a real guy.

## The Power of Listening

My Dad used to say, "Convince a man against his will, he will form the same opinion still." The Bible says, "Let those with ears to hear, hear, and those with eyes to see, see." Very often, people do not want to hear advice, truth, or a good factual observation.

The people who refuse to see or hear like to cling to their description and motive as "perception." If you want to live in a fantasy world, you have every right to. The problem is you will have much disappointment and problems in life. Their conviction on living in the dark gets described as bad luck. Another one is, "This is my cross to bear."

God wants us to live happy and content, not in suffering and confusion. So, be willing to listen and see the message of God through His example of His Son, Jesus Christ, and His life here on Earth. He was sent to teach and instruct us with examples for all of us to hear and see.

## Where Have You Gone?

When someone pulls away
One doesn't know what to say.
Suddenly there is a closing door
And our hearts and minds connect no more.
In life, there is always a time and season
For everything, there is a reason.
When this happens, it is very sad.
How can something so good become so bad?
In comes the mystery and the why.
The puzzlement is so very high.
I keep searching for the key
For that person to once again like me.
It's possible it's something I did or am doing.
I need to know to get back going.
Always be there in plain sight
If the person hasn't taken flight.
For, with time, there may be a change in view
For the person who departed from you.
Where have you gone, that I can't see?
Whither you are, there also I want to be.

## Fact and Theory; Truth and Perception

These two debates are closely connected. One is always real, and the other is either a possibility or imagined. You can always follow fact and truth to a worthwhile conclusion or decision. The other two always tease and bait you into false dreams, expectations, and indecision.

The problem most people have is defining the two debates. Usually, the fact and truth call for more sacrifice or hard work to address the issue at hand. The theory or perception usually tends to be easier, and possibly the result we may favor short-term. Fact and theory always have a foundation or base to build on and grow. The other direction is "well, it might work" or a "good enough, for now" approach. Fact and truth are always present—"seek and you shall find." This is where ambition and research pay off. Conversely, the lazy, risky way results in a lot of disappointment and failure. So, seek the truth wherever it leads you, and you will be given many rewards for it.

## Which One Are You?

There are those who never give up
And those, you can't get up.
Quite a contrast on the go.
One goes fast, the other slow.
Some are always willing and ready.
Others need a push to get moving steady.
When the day is over, one will admire.
The opposite will do enough to tire.
So, look in the mirror, and see which one is you.
If you don't like the answer, you can start over new.

## Some Often Used Sayings

- If you have to ask the price of something, you probably can't afford it.
- Quality remains long after the price is forgotten.
- A friend in need is a pest.
- When you see lots of arrows, and they are all pointing in one direction, follow them.
- Never make a decision out of fear or greed.
- Do not suffer from the paralysis of analysis.
- When you see something that needs to be corrected or righted, and you need to oppose the wrong that is being done, ask yourself this question: What are *you* going to do about it?

- When all is said and done, there is usually more said than done.
- I used to be indecisive, but now I'm not so sure.
- What the fox said when he couldn't reach the grapes: "They were probably sour anyhow."
- "Don't miss the main event because of the side show."
- "He couldn't see the forest for the trees."

## A Balltown Story

In the 1940s, every young man had to have a physical exam for the Army draft. So, one Sunday, after Mass, Father Mauer asked one of these young men who had just returned from such a trip, "Tell me George, where did you go for this exam?" George replied in a typical small town manner, "Father, I don't know if I went North, South, East, or West. All I know is, I went through Chicago."

Another story is about the hog farmer, who unluckily had one of his young hogs hit by a car and killed in his farmyard. He was complaining about this uptown at the local tavern, and another farmer told him he had heard enough, get over it. The first farmer said, "Sure, you got good talking. You have 200 hogs, I only had 12. So, to you, it's just another dead hog, but to me, it meant a lot more."

## Quotes from Priests

- *Wedding homily:* True love means self-sacrifice.
- *Homily, St. Paul Church:* There is no greater sin than to use another human being for your own personal gain.
- *Father Landolt:* On our human years of life: "We are just passing through." On giving to charity: "Individually, it means very little, but collectively, it means a lot." On wedding ceremonies, but also, on life itself: "There is beauty in simplicity."
- *Father Holtzer:* "Joe, you know there is no justice this side of heaven."
- *Father Whalen's procrastinator's creed:* "Never put off till tomorrow what you can avoid altogether."
- *Father Hirsch:* "When you sing, you lift your heart and mind to God."

- *Father Levenhagen:* On dating: "There is an old saying that absence makes the heart grow fonder. When two people are apart, one should add three words to the saying 'for someone else'."
- *Father Kalb:* "Some people come to church only three times in their life: when hatched (Baptism), matched (Marriage), and dispatched (Funeral)."
  - "There are three forms of communication: telegraph, telephone, and tell-a-woman."
  - His advice to a young man who broke up with his girlfriend: "Don't be depressed. Girlfriends are like a bus. There will be another one along any minute."
- *Another story with a lesson:* "A beggar was sitting on the street when an affluent couple walked by. The beggar asked for a donation. The gentleman reached in his pocket and gave him a twenty dollar bill. The wife criticized him saying, 'Why did you do that? You might know he'll just spend it on booze and harm his health further.' The husband replied, 'All I did was offer him a chance and a choice, and that's all any of us are offered in this life. What we do with it is up to us.' So, we are all offered these same two things everyday of our human lives, with our free will."

## Stories and Sayings from My Father

- "Nothing is so lightly spun, that it doesn't reach the light of the sun."
- An old Irish neighbor and friend chatted with my dad one day and exclaimed, "It's a great day for the race." Dad replied, "What race is that?" The neighbor said, "Well, the human race, of course."
- Years ago, my dad's relatives from across the state of Iowa would come for a long visit. As he answered their knock on the door, Dad's cousin would say to him, "I am here to make you happy—either when I come, or when I leave."
- About someone who had unrealistic expectations about a venture: "He thought the fried pigeons were going to fly right into his mouth."
- From the Bible: "Pride cometh before the fall."
- Story with a moral: "Mike and Pat met in the field one day. Says Mike to Pat, 'I see you have a nice shiny pocket watch in your bibs.' Pat says, 'Oh yes, my son gave it to me for my birthday.'

Mike asks, 'By the way, what time is it?' Pat pulls out the watch and shows it to Mike and says 'There she is,' and Mike replies, 'Damned if she ain't.' Neither knew how to tell time. The moral of the story is: Many times we have something worthwhile in life, but we aren't wise enough or smart enough to learn how to use it."

- My dad was chatting with another about fishing and asked the man if he ever saw a catfish. "Of course" was the reply, "I sure did." Then my dad asked, "How did he hold the pole?"
- "Look for trouble, and you'll find it. How often in life do we create problems when they weren't there before? Get positive, and stay positive."
- "Don't talk about money. It makes me nervous." (This tells me finances were quite secondary in his priorities in life.)
- The story of the rich king: "The court jester, who performed for the king one day, asked the king if he could look in the vault with all the gold and treasures of the king. The king agreed, and opened the vault door so the jester could see in. The jester proclaimed, after a brief look, 'Well your majesty, I am now just as rich as you are.' The king asked, 'Why do you feel that way?' The jester reasoned, 'Because I looked and saw your fortune, and that is all you ever do with it. You never use it for any good for the people of your kingdom.'"
- "He thought his nest was feathered." (A comment he made about someone who thought he had married into riches, but found out differently.)

## My Uncle, Monsignor Anthony Sigwarth

- "Often times the preparation and anticipation is nearly as enjoyable as the event itself."
- "In marriage, it isn't 50–50 percent, but rather 100–100 percent."
- "I'm all for Catholic priests being allowed to marry, as long as they don't make it mandatory."
- A middle school student was participating in a school play, and he was given one line to learn. As the sound effects sounded a loud bang, he was to exclaim, "Hark, I hear a cannon." He practiced and practiced, and on the performance of the play, he reacted to

the loud bang by jumping and declaring, "What the hell was that noise?" Moral: How often in life do we prepare and angst over a coming event only to be shocked and surprised and sometimes confused when the time comes? Let us stay focused in life.

## My Responses to a Critic on My Parenting

I will take all the blame now, but I also want all of the credit later. We don't raise children. We raise crops, animals, and foodstuffs on the farm. We teach children. We teach and nurture them by our words and our example, so we should be aware of these at all times.

### Incentive

Some days when you hit the wall
Turn it around, and have a ball.
Seek some enjoyment of body and mind.
Make sure it is of the healthy kind.
A movie, music, a book would be fine.
Also a gourmet meal with some wine.
If available, do this with a friend
And for sure your spirit will mend.
Now that you have the recipe
Go out and make yourself happy.

## The Surprise

My, are people surprised when they see the results of believing. Faith is believing in what is really there. The doubt factor is so puzzling and mysterious to the human psyche. We know and want what is real, and yet we give in to the temptation of doubting. We neutralize it! Often, it comes from others who question us and our real beliefs, but sometimes, we entertain it ourselves. This is because we don't have the glue of self-confidence that comes with the repetition of successful thinking and action. We allow ourselves to become sidetracked by the queries of multiple doubters who often surround us.

Build a shell of armor to the negative approach when there isn't a negative. Protect yourself from the unreal suggestions of your critics and naysayers. This is a constant go-round because of the faction of people who automatically disagree. It is always "we" and "them," and never "us" in a discussion or debate. Think and act on your beliefs and knowledge, and you won't become the recipient of surprise.

You know, and I know, so spread the know.

## Lonely

Today, I feel very alone.
Sad, because of all the love I've shown.
Misunderstood, or taken for granted.
Always given straight, and never planted.
Most people are guarded or protected.
Others are very often neglected.
I'm here, the same, with a large heart.
But not allowed to play the same part.
The message is: you are not needed anymore.
Can do it by myself, what do I need you for?
Possibly, it's time to go where I'm known
Like the bird who from the nest has flown
To the realm where only love survives.
Where understanding and warmth is in all their lives
Because they embraced and learned each.
I may choose to stay and teach
And tolerate being sometimes alone.
For there is a need in those not grown
To have the seeds of love sown.

## Two People Came Together

A father and his son were having a serious talk about their relationship. The son felt somewhat apart, and distanced. The father went on to explain all the things in life he had provided for the son, such as supporting him through school, and also a degree in mechanical drafting. "I helped you find the school you wanted. I helped you find a car so you had transportation, and I was always there when you needed me." The son replied, "I know, Dad, but where were you when I didn't need you?" Tears formed in their eyes, and they had a compassionate hug. They became much closer at that moment, and remained that way. Sometimes, the right words at the right time have the impact we desire in understanding each other. I witnessed this myself, and was quite touched. Please talk to each other, and also listen when you have feelings that aren't settled or comfortable. The result can be quite fruitful.

## Cooperation

The spirit of cooperation is one of the important ingredients in a family situation, as well as in the workplace. I feel it must be difficult to explain or describe, because I have found few people who actually understand it. So, I will make one more attempt at it.

Cooperation is needed for success in any group that shares a common goal, such as a family, work, team sports, and whole communities. Lots of times, cooperation is demanded by our employers, family members, or teammates. Sometimes, a contract is in place, or it is a requirement for future participation. Now, I see this often comes to "whether you *have* to or whether you *want* to."

The "want to" part always has the best results. This is because the spirit involved leads to a fuller or fullest application of our abilities in the area we are involved in. Sayings from the past supporting this are, "You are either with me or against me." "All for one, and one for all." Or, "I can tell your heart just wasn't in it. You sure did a half-assed job of it." Therefore, it comes down to the question of what do we bring to the table, not only in ability, but in the spirit of cooperation.

Every act we do that requires cooperation will produce either positive or negative, constructive or destructive, helpful or harmful, inspiring or depressive, energizing or tiresome, progressive or delaying, harmony or dissent, efficient or wasteful contributions to our effective goal. Consider the contrasts and decide which ones appeal to you, and then, ask yourself, "Which spirit will I choose to live in?" Put this spirit in the drive position, and enjoy the harmony that life offers.

## Valuable

Our body needs a good rest.
Every night this gets put to the test.
Sometimes, we have a very deep slumber
And it sounds as if we are sawing lumber.
We strive for a sleep of peace and serenity.
In times of stress, this is a scarce entity.
So, be calm as you drop off to sleep.
Put your worries aside, they will keep.
And, to a world of good dreams you'll go
To renew your body from head to toe.
Find many ways to make this unfold.
For the value of good sleep is worth more than gold.

## Politics

Politics have been around as long as people ruled over others. Kingships and emperors ruled in ancient times, and now dictators and democracies share in global politics. Some of the descriptions of politics are oppression, class difference, and lots of corruption. The one thing they all lack is truth.

Truth helps communicate reality to the people of a country. When we identify what is actually happening, we have a good chance of solving problems. The lies perpetrated on us wield tremendous power for those who manipulate them. With the power go greed, wealth, and profit. Also, many truthful people are intimidated and silenced by either bribes or blackmail. This is a huge mess. The environment is terribly vicious.

This condition will not change until a large group in Congress weighs in at one time, and has the truth behind and with them to turn things around. A "Truth Party" is what we need to lead the people to prosperity, and a comfortable attitude towards fellow citizens. The power of the vote is still here. Research and study the candidates, and cast an informed vote for the person of your choice. Please don't simply vote the party, or the family background of a candidate. You owe much more to yourself and to your country. Remember, Truth is successful.

## Words

Words are the most used and the most abused (misapplied) tool we have in our communication opportunity. They are often used for spin and personal attack instead of being used in a descriptive and accurate intention. There is truth in all words, so it is wise to find and know what these truths are. Then, you can use words for their maximum value, and enjoy the impact they have.

People who are too lazy to do this end up being poorly expressed and misunderstood much of the time. Right away, they start blaming the other party in a conversation when this takes place, calling them narrow-minded, unreceptive, and even stupid.

No communication exists. But, all along, they are the ones who lack the ability to match proper and truthful words to the meaning they are trying to convey. Proper words have a clarity and vision to those saying them, as well as to anyone who is willing to listen, and to identify with them. Communication is always a two-way street, but a sincere attempt to use the right words will be a success.

## Leave of Absence

It's called a leave of absence.
More like a leave of presence.
Can't decide whether you're in or out.
Seems like there is a lot of doubt.
But I can see the merit of it all.
It is about life coming to a stall.
The pace will slow and become bearable
And life will become more charitable.
So, if you need to be removed from the scene
Consider the escape that isn't mean.
You can come back all rejuvenated
And also much more motivated
To carry on the task of your life's work.
And to those who look at you and smirk,
Say to them, "I was gone for a while.
Now I'm back to make you smile."

## Live Forward

Have you noticed how many people are very fond of reminiscing about past events in their lives? Especially if one is near the elderly years of earthly life. Sure, it feels good and warm to remember the good times in life that were successful and happy, and sometimes we embellish them. I had a close relative who changed his story a little each time he told it in order to shape it in the way he wished it had actually happened.

I find it more fulfilling to live present time, and look forward to the future transition to the life awaiting us at our human passing. Let us use the learning experience we had to do good in people's lives as long as we are able.

The first step is to understand our exchange in life is close, and each moment and day can have a positive approach, and a mutual reward. Opportunities are all around us wherever we are, and no matter what physical condition we are in.

Let us seek and recognize them, so we can learn and grow even more now, and in the future, than in the past. Let us not sit idle and revel in our accomplishments, or feel sorry for our missed chances. Because the ones nearest and now are the sweetest gift we are being offered daily. Shall we harvest the now, or try to redo the days gone by?

This is our chance, and our choice.

## The "A" Words

Some of the most meaningful words about a relationship with God are "A" words.

I start with "aware." Awareness is necessary to see or visualize the awesome love and magnitude of God that are shown to us in all of creation. If we are not aware of its existence, we will never experience the joy of its intention.

Now, if we are aware, and recognize this unending gift, we must welcome it into our lives, and "allow" it to nourish and satisfy our spirits. We need to open the door to our hearts and souls, and invite this energy of life to come in.

After we have hosted and entertained this spiritual joy and sustenance, the next step is to "abide" with this Love that is without end.

I surely like the "A" words. How about giving them a try?

## Sunday Morning

The sky is blue and the sun is shining.
There could never be a better timing
To get in touch with beauty as such.
There is none as great, not near as much.
Words alone cannot describe
The joy of the moment that is so alive.
The freshness of the air, the warmth of the sun
Is nature showing us it cannot be overcome.
It is there for us to enjoy each time.
And furthermore, it doesn't cost a dime.
Next morning, look up and see
What is there to allow in ecstasy.

## Support

One of the things I enjoy most in life is support. I enjoy giving it as well as receiving it. In today's selfish me-ism attitude in our society, whether family or work or a team situation, it is a welcome feeling because of the rewards it gives. Many of us have felt alone when facing a problem or difficult task until some kind person gave their personal support. When the opposite happens, such as criticism or opposition, it has a very cruel result. Support can be given in many ways, such as physical, moral, or financial. These are all ways of helping another when there is a true need. These are also given in varying degrees. Remember, they all count and help to build strength. As the Texans like to say, "You are either with me or agin me." So, don't forget, standing passively by is not an option. It is a way of being against, by omission. Stand up tall and strong in supporting the people and ideals you believe in, and try to teach and show by example those who don't.

## Face Up

We all face many difficult situations in life, some material, but most in relationships. We have several paths to take when these arise. Most people find ways to avoid a solution or understanding because it will require a great deal of effort and unselfishness. Do we make the effort for a personal outcome, or do we seek a dual understanding and acceptance? It can't be always only about me. So many people end up just walking away, or hiding from a solution, but, lo and behold, another dilemma will pop-up soon. Once you learn to come together in some fashion, the next occurrence will be much easier. Another path is to escalate and aggravate the situation in hopes the other person will give up or walk away. This path is very destructive to all involved, and causes further pain. I'd like to add that time is always an ally, as it helps to soften feelings and allows for understanding and awareness of what is really happening. Each occasion has its own circumstances, but the unselfishness base you need to have will result in a good ending. I recommend to "face up", and not "mask up."

## Go, Go, Go

Why are we always in a hurry
And do everything in a flurry?
Instead of a nice steady pace
We act like we are in a race.
So, do your work in a competent way
And in the long run, it will pay.
When we do things without a frown
The blood pressure will go down.
Pace yourself, and your health you'll save
To prevent arrival of an early grave.

## Parenting Approach

Parents often stress about raising children. First off, I disagree with the term "raising." I prefer teaching, by word and example, and also the word "guiding." One raises crops, gardens, animals, and even a flag. Children are much more superior and precious to us, and so are our relationships with them. Descriptions of parenting are such words as: discipline, punishment, rewards, and rules. Most of these tend to make parents and children adversaries. Adding to this is the difficulty of communicating properly with children. Parents want their children to act according to the way the parents want them to. Children have ideas and visions of their own, that should be recognized, respected, and considered. What seems small and trivial to parents can appear huge and insurmountable to a child. If actions are harmful to the child, this needs to be communicated in a way that the child can understand and accept.

Even crying, by young children, is a way for them to communicate. They are letting us know they are unhappy or mournful with their situation. This is where guidance is needed. Guide them in an explanation that can be understood by them. If the first one fails, keep going until you feel a reception from the child. When parents act stern and rigid, the children instinctively feel fearful and overwhelmed, as well as frustrated. So, to guide with a gentle heart and hand has the greatest outcome when disagreements appear.

Once children sense you are working together, each time or occurrence will become easier. Key words to remember are: guidance, communication, and gentleness.

Also, if the environmental situation is the cause or block to a solution, remove the environment. Change it to a different location, different stimulus, different attitude.

Do I guarantee these things will work every time? Hell, no. But, a great deal of the time, you will find success and a happy relationship with your child. One final note to all parents: "Don't try too hard." Sometimes you need to back up, calm down, and let time be your ally.

## Sit Awhile

Did you ever get in a rut,
Have that empty feeling in your gut?
Don't know which plan to cut?
Maybe just bend down, and pet the mutt.
This doesn't solve your melancholy.
What you need is some folly.
To make you laugh and feel jolly.
A drink with a friend would be good, by golly.
Play some music and stories do share.
Get in a mood, so you don't care
About all the work you look at and stare.
Feeling fine in your comfy chair.
When your work is always constant, we call it a break.
These times, we often do not take.
The demands are such, much is at stake.
But, to keep going, set aside time, we must make.

## Learning

Be careful what you learn. You may choose to live that life. We now have the path to expand and grow. Of course, responsibilities come when you enter the gate. It is a good feeling to be responsible for a happier, more fulfilled life. We are now partnering with our common goal, which, by the way, has no limits. It is enjoyable to learn and grow, and this path accelerates as we go. So, remove the roadblocks with your newly found enlightenment, and look for some passengers to take along on the journey.

### Changing Times

When all seems doom and gloom,
Good things will come soon.
Nothing stays the same.
There is sunshine, and then there is rain.
This too will pass, that's for sure.
When there is sickness, always a cure.
Often times, we have to wait
For the pain to be gone on that date.
Without faith, it may not take place.
With hope, the smile will be back on our face.
So I will carry on with or without a song
Because I know the change will not be long.
It will come much sooner than never
And there will be happiness and peace forever.

## I'll Take the Job

When looking for someone to hire
They must be willing to perspire,
Keep focused and concentrate
So no injury would be your fate.
Always have a good attitude
And the boss will show gratitude.
Working together is a two-way street.
So always be ready to move your feet.
Be sure to work with integrity.
This will lead to job longevity.
The boss was giving a man an interview
To see and judge how he would do.
Before the wage was discussed, how high?
"I'll take the job," was his reply.

## Sanctity of Life

Why is it that people who have life, and spend thousands and thousands of dollars to maintain and repair their health, think it is acceptable to end the life of unborn babies on demand? I know this way of life and death is wrong and deplorable. We cling to every procedure and medication that prolongs our own lives, and yet allow the procedure of abortion to end someone else's life. This is not only hypocritical, it is dead wrong. No pun intended.

Many also spend huge sums of money to promote and save the lives of their pets, and yet promote the choice to abort life in the form of human babies. Animal rights activists protect the safety and humane treatment of animals (which they deserve), and yet allow human danger and inhumane treatment in the form of murder to innocent and helpless babies to go on daily.

Where do these people's priorities lie? They seem to live in a selfish hell of denial and have a total lack of respect for human life. We who see the truth in the hardened errors of "pro-choice" stance have a responsibility and a choice to speak out as often and forcefully as possible to defend and save the sanctity of life. Abortion, as it is carried out around the world, is like a boat heading for a waterfall of despair, instead of choosing to board the ocean-liner of life.

## Credit

In accounting, we are all familiar with the terms credit and debit. They are used all the time with bank card transactions and ledger sheets. It seems to me, in life we are all too often ready to debit or blame ourselves, whenever things or plans don't go right. This usually happens to go on for a long time, and it uses up a lot of our good energy. Once you recognize a mistake, study it, learn from it, and then, *let it go*. The credit part of this comparison is seldom, if ever, used. Something good happens due to our effort and completion, and all we feel is that we had it coming. This event was overdue. Here is where credit is due and we need to apply it to ourselves. A simple pat on the back is a good start. Also, a reflection of what happened and how it came about is beneficial. It adds to our account of knowledge and experience, and we are richer and have more equity to build on. Please don't feel egotistical about these things, but rather be thankful and grateful for a job well done or a goal reached.

### Staying Home

There is a lot to be said about staying home.
First of all, it removes your urge to roam.
At home, you can always be comfortable
And it is also much more affordable.
Some look forward to their next vacation.
I look forward to the next good meal at the plantation.
At home, you can sit in your chair with comfort.
After a while the pain will no longer hurt.
You can make yourself a drink at your own bar.
You can get your glow without going far.
Ostracism in your social life will fall.
Why should that be, when all your friends are on the wall.
So consider the option of closing the door
And enjoying life even more.
When you are away, you sleep in a strange bed.
You could be home getting a "sleep" instead.

## Childhood

My dad had a saying he repeated to me: "Once a man, and twice a child." He was referring to the physical aspect of life. True to his saying, Dad's life ended in a hospital bed for the last year, unable to feed himself, and in need of constant care just like a newborn child. His picture was played out as he saw it.

Also, in scriptures: "Unless you become like a child, you cannot enter the kingdom of heaven." We enter this human world created in perfection, and are in a state of truth and love and peace. We go through life, and face many illusions and confrontations as we learn and grow. As we search and find our way back to where we started as a child, we have the opportunity and mission to help others with our message of truth and respect that we have become aware of.

So, I see Dad's saying being played out in both physical and spiritual realms. Let us seek the purity of new creation and look for it in others as we live our daily lives.

## The Calendar

The calendar begins and ends with lots of cheer.
It is the human measure of a year.
It's made up of days and dates
To make sure we're scheduled to not be late.
Anniversaries, birthdays, and holidays
All make for a colorful page.
As each month of the year comes off
Sometimes too fast, fast as a cough.
Let us slow down the pace.
Treat each day face to face.
To do as much good as we are able
Like a hearty meal on our table.
And like a real fine wine,
Taste and enjoy the calendar time.

## Habits

The definition of habit is to do something over and over until we do it without even realizing it. When we have good habits, we seem to enjoy the results and have a happier life.

Most of our good habits in life happen because we have learned them, through the years, from people who are or were our role models. This is always our free choice to follow those people's examples and lifestyles and beliefs. This is why it is important for young people to be near or exposed to some "good habits" people, and shown the difference between these and others who routinely display bad habits.

Bad habits result in a less safe, harmful environment. We are then exposed to injury, pain, and suffering in our physical selves as well as our emotional and character selves.

I implore all parents, teachers, coaches, and leaders to help young people find suitable role models, and to build meaningful relationships with others. The children of today become the leaders of tomorrow. Let us hope they lead with good habits and example, and not negative temptations to show us the sad, sorrowful side of life.

## Finances

My dad always said: "Talking about money makes me nervous"
This is a subject that may seem a curse.
Why is it something so necessary
Becomes so very, very contrary
To our natural instinct and needs?
Lead some to be overcome with greed.
They become obsessed with satisfaction
That is fed with a monetary distraction.
It draws all these to believe
In a false value you will never receive.
So search for obsessions you will always strive
And you will start the path that will cause you to drive
Straight into an empty reservoir
There to dwell forever more.

## What Are You Doing Today?

When discussing issues about life and current events, most people are very sure and willing to tell you what they have done or are planning to do about them. Very rarely is anyone sure or excited about what they are doing right now about it. Thus, my question: "What are you doing to address the issue today?" Today is when things happen, not yesterday's past or tomorrow's future. Each morning, we should identify and address the highest priority need with all of our energy. Sometimes, the answer of what to do about it is to get more information and knowledge in order to make a correct decision. This is fine, and is not putting it off. It is when we shelve or table things that nothing happens. So, I invite you and myself to be more focused and aggressive in solving problems, and also finding joyous events in today's living.

### The Great Event

Every year in January time
A huge event gets many on the starting line.
People come from all over the country for the race.
A marathon it is, so don't forget to pace.
Running gives us such a good feeling.
The endorphins send us reeling
To a much higher consciousness level.
To a place where you won't find the devil.
Some folks view running as an affliction.
I refer to it as a positive addiction.
The race is similar to human life.
Has a beginning and an end, along with some strife.
The satisfaction and reward are high at completion.
Drink lots of liquids to avoid fluid depletion.
But when you come to the last mile
You can look back and feel good with a wide smile.
To those who are here, it is great to be alive.
End the day and the stay with lots of high fives.

## Child Psychology

In a conversation with a parent recently, he commented, "I am not a child psychologist." I believe he definitely is, because he is a parent, and that requires you to be one. The relationship with the mind and behavior of your child is individual and unique. There are no two exactly the same. Many times, it is easy to give generic advice to other parents than to take the responsibility of finding the path or channel of communication with each of your individual children. Both the parent and the child richly deserve this. This foundation of understanding may be enjoyed for a lifetime. Understanding does not always lead to agreement, and this is when the instinctive, natural "child psychologist" in you is needed. It will be there, if you are willing to recognize it and use it. The mind and behavior of a child are reaching out to us parents for guidance and learning. All parents should be generous and open to provide everything they possess to further the growth of their children's hearts and characters.

## Trinity

Two sisters came from the Southeast and the Southwest
To meet with another in Iowa no less.
Good visiting, good wine, and good meals
Make the gathering so very ideal.
They remove stress by sharing joy and laughter.
After all, isn't this what, in life, we are after?
This is an annual event here in the cold.
One whole week together, when all else is on hold.
One says it helps her to motivate.
Another finds it causes her to rejuvenate.
They are all for one, and stick together.
If the man in the house disagrees, he soon knows better.
So he embraces the tribunal with its beauty and splendor
And all the good times are cherished and remembered.

## Vision

Vision is a very interesting word. It describes your ability to see and how well it functions. It also means to have a picture or plan for the future, so you can work to achieve this goal or wish. These two meanings are very related, as if you can see things realistically in the present, it will help you greatly to fulfill your future vision. Conversely, if you see things falsely or imagined, that is as far as your so-called vision will ever go. It is good to give yourself a vision test periodically to see if you are seeing the roots and results of reality satisfactorily. Life has a way of pulling us away from the facts at times. As the words in a line from a song say, "I can see clearly now." Strive to keep the clarity constant. This will help us to keep our vision of eternity peaceful, joyous, happy, and fulfilled.

## Mental Block

"Convince a man against his will, he will form the same opinion still," is an old saying of my father that rings true so often today. Think of how many times you tried to teach, inform, clarify, warn, instruct, or simply tried to help someone, and the help was totally refused by their mental block. There are many reasons for this, and none of them are worthwhile or creditable. Here are some of the responses: "What the hell does he know?" or "Whatever," or "That S.O.B isn't going to tell me what to do," or "They are just telling me that for their own gain." This is quite frustrating for the good people who are compassionate, educated, intelligent, and knowledgeable about the subject, whether it is in business, health related, or even in spiritual matters. Some of the things that make up the mental block are: pride, ignorance, apathy, stubbornness, arrogance, and just plain hostility. People like this don't know, don't care to know, like to resist everything, think they are as wise as or wiser than everyone else, and just plain want to argue about anything. Someday each person will become aware and be enlightened and satisfied with truth and advice. Let us hope it is sooner rather than later in life.

## Guidance

When we are a child
We start out meek and mild.
We look for approval as we grow
So that our self-worth isn't too low.
For confidence is necessary in those formative years
To prevent a whole lot of tears.
To believe in oneself is so needed.
Be careful not to become conceited.
Always remain as the child in your heart
Because, after all, it is your best part.
As you grow older and have children of your own
Don't forget the past lessons you've known.
You can sort the right from wrong
And use it in family all day long.
Remember who you were and who you are.
This balance will take you far.
This understanding will help you pass it on
To the next and the next generation.

## Success

Nothing succeeds like success! Many of us set out to succeed on a daily basis. Of course, one of the roads to success is to set attainable and reasonable goals. We all know our abilities and limits, so it is wise to stay within ourselves. In other words, don't be a dreamer of the impossible. We all have plenty of these skills to work with and play with in an enjoyable fashion. Success is always more satisfying when it is inclusive instead of exclusive. When our success touches other people's lives, we become rewarded from many, and not just one. Success is often complemented by the contribution of others, and the network continues to grow. So, stay confident, stay motivated, and work with an energy deserving of the task. This will lead to not only success in the current endeavor, but also success in the relationships of those who surround us, and those we come in contact with.

## Sports

Life is filled with comparisons or analogies with situations in sporting events. Each morning is "batter up" for the opportunity to take a swing at the human pitch coming our way. Sometimes, there is a curve ball coming our way to adjust to.

The concept of team effort can relate to family life and also the workplace. We have the stars in games who excel and win, and we also have players who choke in stressful situations, and give in to the fear of failing. This tells us to live with full confidence in ourselves and the fact that we control the outcomes of our daily lives.

Lots of terms come to mind, such as a "slam dunk," meaning that you can't miss scoring the goal. Of course, there is the "grand slam," when four runs are scored with one coordinated swing of the bat. Also, "crossing the finish line," whether in a race or scoring a touchdown, relates to successfully reaching goals that we set. So, sports set a good example for us to be confident, disciplined, focused, and cooperative in our daily lives.

### January in Iowa

The cold is nearly unbearable.
It is very close to swear-able.
Each night, the temp drops below zero degrees.
Makes my whole body shiver, even my knees.
We have but two choices, adapt or complain.
I'd rather adapt, and alleviate the pain.
For once we accept the conditions around us,
We find a way to co-exist without any of the fuss.
Isn't this what life is all about?
A lesson learned to help us out.
So dress up extra warm
To keep your body from harm.
Take each day of cold to do some learning
And stop for June and July the yearning.
For it will come in six months or so
And you will forget the winter that had to go.

## Controversy

It is my experience in life, that each time a controversial issue comes along, it becomes very exaggerated, and therefore, more severe than necessary. The first mistake is to tell many more people about it than need to know. Naturally, the talk and gossip multiply and magnify the problem. It becomes so entwined and large, that a confrontation is usually inevitable. Confrontation, at the wrong time, leads to a sure fight, which becomes distracted and personal many times. This seldom leads to a solution. Timing of discussion and debate on the issue is of the utmost importance. Allow enough time for those involved to lighten up and have a better perspective. Hopefully, emotions will soften, and all parties become better listeners. All this is important if the parties involved really want to reach a mutual agreement. If this factor isn't present, all of the above advice is futile. It is so necessary to not poison the water before addressing the problem that exists. So, know patience and willingness if you really want to resolve controversy.

## Actions

Every act we do is done in either a responsible or irresponsible manner. I'll talk about responsibility at another time. Today, it is action. Actions have consequences. How often we hear that phrase today. Sure they do, but I am observing way too many instances of inaction. "I'm going to do this" or "I'm going to do the other thing." Well, nothing ever got done by "going to." Things get accomplished by action, by doing. Nike's famous commercial phrase is, "Just do it."

Also, a lot of our actions are reactive rather than proactive. We wait until we are forced to act, and then we respond. Why play defense all the time? Play offense and seize the thought or plan and work at the completion and satisfaction of it.

Stay focused and disciplined while performing any task for maximum results. Always strive for ambition and action rather than apathy and procrastination. This also sets a good example for your family and for co-workers as well. It will also help to draw the "action" out of others.

## The Fixer

Oh, if only I could create
It would be one to fix, and do it first rate.
It seems that almost every day
Something needs attention right away.
A decision to make, what and where
To solve the problem at which I stare.
I know this is part of everyday farming.
As for peace of mind, it is very harming.
I look forward to when there is someone else to ask.
Here it is, your fixing task.
Not only will I have peace of mind
But life, to me, will be much more kind.

## Focus

One of the main ideas to remember when solving problems or achieving goals is to stay focused. Our society is disillusioned with all of the stimuli of marketing, advertising, and saturation of visuals and products. The promise of a "quick fix" or "an easy way" often proves to be disappointing. It is important to have an open mind, and at the same time, a determined sense of direction. The path we take should always be constructive, reasonable, and achievable. There is also a moral aspect to this situation. How will our actions and direction affect others—the people around us, and those whose lives may be touched by them? This is another huge reason to stay focused on our goals and our motives. Our intentions should be honorable as well as profitable. "What does it profit a man if he gaineth the whole world, but loseth his soul?" So, keep your aim at the important things in life, and avoid the distractions that are constantly around you. Stay focused!

## Kodak Moment

Each phase of our human life is a snapshot of our actions and accomplishments. At or near the end of this time, how will our photo albums look to us and others? The beautiful part of this is we can add to or create wonderful pictures each moment we are here. What legacy have we left for others, and what more do we want to build? By occasionally looking at our albums to date, we can see where we have connected with people for the good of all, and we can see where we missed. We have a chance to fill in these misses as we continue our daily adventure. I urge you to become the sculptor in shaping your relationships with everyone you come in contact with. By shaping your future in this positive approach, you can fill that photo album with lots of lessons learned and experiences to pass on to whoever cares to look and relate to them. How we live today does matter to us and others in far more ways than we actually realize. Therefore, remember the camera is always aimed at us, ready to capture our deeds and misdeeds. Be loving and considerate of the posterity you leave to us.

## Who Is to Say?

This time in my life, poems are what I do.
For me, this is something brand new.
It's fun to write some chatter.
The subject doesn't really matter
Because there is something to say
About each and every day
As well as the people we know and love.
Of our friends and family we never get tired of.
As stories and humor abound
The laughter is such a nice sound.
So I'll keep writing them until I'm told
That is for people who are senile and old.
But my reply is: "They are there for all."
"I'll continue because I'm having a ball."

## Perseverance

This is a word with lots of synonyms such as stubborn, strong-willed, tenacious, and even bull-headed. To persevere can be a very attractive strength, and also a character flaw at other times. To use it to reach a responsible goal is quite complimentary, as well as when you are in a struggle for a good cause. Learning and maintaining good habits in order to regain proper health status is also a time to persevere vigorously in that area. Surely, in life, there are times when our goals will be denied, but it shouldn't be the result of giving up.

Always live by the motto: "Don't ever, ever, ever give up." This means our goals weren't achieved because of factors we could not control, rather than a failure to give it our best shot. It is always important to recognize when this is. The more we persevere, the stronger our characters become, with increased self-confidence and self-esteem.

To find a partner in life who shares this ambition and passion can lead to a whole family of achievers who teach all of the people their lives touch. Grab onto the "never, ever give up" mentality, and follow the path that it leads you on.

## Transition

We are all facing a transition from our human life to our next one. The question for each one of us is: "How will this be for me?" A lot depends on how we live now, and what our priorities are. Are we moving closer to a smooth or peaceful transition, or to a rough and fearful one? How high is our awareness or consciousness level? Have we grown, and are we continuing to grow along this path, or have we become complacent and stagnant, waiting for this event to happen to us? Have our material goals consumed our energy so that there is little available for our spiritual advancement? Let us not lament the past, but rather look ahead to the future. Transition means going from the old to the new. Examples are: going from one job to another, going from one airline to another during travel, going from childhood to mature adulthood. As we visualize these examples, we should ask ourselves: "How am I handling this transition into my next level of residence?"

## Time Out

These words are used to stop the action during a sporting event. They are used to discipline children when needed. There are many more uses, such as time out of your day to do something out of your usual routine. This is a convenient way to stop the hectic and confusing times in our lives. I feel this is very beneficial for us to get a rest, or to get a new perspective on a situation. It also helps us to reflect and plan a way forward at times of an unwelcome occurrence. This is a very good tool to say, "Whoa. Let us renew and regroup our thoughts and our feelings and our lives." So, periodically, let us take time out for a "time out" and enjoy the benefits this opportunity provides us with.

## Batter Up

Each day of life we step up to the plate.
Better show up and don't be late.
Be ready to take your swing
Or you may miss everything.
Miss the things in life that are small
But on priorities, hit the ball.
Hitting is part of offense, so keep that in mind
When in comes a pitch of every kind.
Be thankful for opportunity of each morning you live.
When the umpire yells "Batter Up," give it all you have to give.

## Depression

How many people today get diagnosed with depression or feel depressed? First of all, depression is not a sickness or disease, but rather the result of depressing. Why do so many of us depress? I attribute this to learned behavior. From an early age, we must struggle to have self-confidence and self-esteem. It begins when we hear words like, "You are a bad boy or girl." Seldom do we hear the words that are needed, "You are a good boy or girl." The good comment is mostly forgotten or taken for granted. Then we start school, and we are severely graded on our work and knowledge. Does the grade we receive ever match up to our hopes and expectations? Rarely. So now we have a reason to depress. In family decisions, when children offer their views, they are usually told, "What do you know? You're just a kid."

The next stage in life, tremendous peer pressure comes into play. We are teenagers and young adults being measured by every classmate and every friend. This can be very stressful and disabling to some. We move on to the age of dating, and sometimes rejection by a member of the opposite sex for no understandable reason. Doubt becomes a major factor in our lives. Fear comes into play because we are now afraid of another relationship. This same pattern joins together often times in our first job. The whole spectrum of the past has now become active as a monster if we allow it.

First and foremost, believe in yourself. You are good and you have ability, and you know this to be true, more than any other living person. Don't ever, ever forget this. Once you have discarded the criticism of others as ignorance instead of fact, you are on a good path. Remember, each morning, you have the chance to have as successful a day as you are willing to allow. Sure, you must apply yourself and your skills, but while you are doing that, there isn't much time left to depress. So, if people around you forget to tell you good things and praise you, be bold enough to tell yourself, because after all, who knows better than you if actions are good, successful, satisfactory, meaningful, and fulfilling? It is always helpful to have this reinforced by others, but don't wait for them to grow your confidence and esteem that is your responsibility. Believe, and you will receive.

## Friend or Foe

They must have invented the cell phone
So no one ever has to be alone.
These gadgets sure come in handy
When you are in trouble, they are dandy.
You call someone and summon rescue
To save your life, and often do.
Other times, it is just a nuisance.
You get calls and texts that don't make sense.
Makes me wonder what will be next
When people are bored with only a text.
Science and technology seem to have no parameters.
It makes the inventions of the past for amateurs.
Hang on and see what the future may bring.
As for me, I'm happy without anything.

## The "B" Words

After a conversation with a family member this morning, I realized the hurt and dilemma these "B" words cause: They are Blame, Bitterness and Bad. Blame is used many times by people when something undesirable happens. We *BLAME* either the situation or the timing or the person we hold responsible for our unhappy event. Usually it is all three that receive our wrath. This leads to the feeling of *BITTERNESS* and we exhibit it in our entire personality and interaction with others. This display is very toxic to our happiness as well as to others. Instead, we need to address the unpleasant occurrence with courage, responsibility and solution. A good question for us is, "How can I learn and grow from this?" *BAD* is the outcome from giving the blame and feeling bitter if we don't remedy this habit. I advise to look to ourselves for control of something we certainly didn't invite. Why this happened isn't as important as what we are going to do about it. So let go of the blame game. Next, being bitter only aggravates the present situation and will continue even longer if we let it. Bitterness leads to anger, jealousy, and misery. Let it go. No one wants to live like that. Bad is all of the above and can be turned into peace and harmony for us and for those around us when we Let It Go.

## Expressing Your Individuality

When our youngest daughter Katie would act out as a young child, critics (or so-called advice counselors) would say, "You are spoiling that child." My response was always, "Let Katie be, she is just expressing her individuality." At the time, I didn't understand the wisdom this carries. It is a natural instinct for a child to explore, expose, and offer themselves to us. It is our task to hear, listen, and accept their individual and unique personality and spirit. It is similar to allowing a flower to bud and bloom, and a bird to hatch and to learn to fly. If this natural process is allowed to advance freely, the intended and complete outcome will occur. My advice is, "Don't get in the way of nature and its evolving process." This is a beautiful event and allowing it to happen is both the music and the dance. Our Katie is now thirty-four years old and has a wonderful husband and two lovely children—a girl and a boy. The scene is again reset, as these children of the new generation ask us to allow them to "Express their Individuality."

## Offense or Defense

Much of our lives, we are told what not to do. We can start with the Ten Commandments. Nearly all of them start out with the words "Thou shalt not…" As children we hear, "Don't do this," Don't do that." This negative approach suppresses us and instills fear about the outcome of our actions. This also leads to temptation in some situations. If told not to do something, people like to explore and find out why. Sometimes, young people take this command as a challenge or a dare when they are among their peers.

I believe in the suggestion, "A good offense is your best defense." By introducing positives as a path to satisfaction and enjoyment, you are allowing young people to express themselves in a free and more complete spirit and manner. When doing this, the drag or resistance of an experience is removed and the positives are allowed to flourish. When exploring new frontiers in our lives, follow the offense of dos and not the defense of don'ts. Have enough confidence in yourself to know that the dos are fruitful and the don'ts are destructive. A simple example is: "Love your neighbor," compared to: "Don't hurt your neighbor."

## Look Up, Lift Up

I just attended a gathering where prayer began and ended the event. A thoughtful observation occurred to me as these prayers took place. Most of the people praying had their heads bowed. Now if I hadn't looked up to see this, I wouldn't have known this fact. I ask, "Why do we have the habit of bowing our heads when praying?"

Praying is talking or communicating with someone else—namely, our Creator and All Loving Spirit. When we human beings speak to one another, it is an insult or disrespect to look down and not engage in a face-to-face conversation. Don't we owe the same respect and engagement to the Being that we are praying to? Would we conduct business or connect with another in a material way if they wouldn't look at us? The real God is our friend, our role model in Jesus Christ, our family, and most importantly, our relative. Our relationship with God is eternal. Why do we bow our heads in prayer? God does not exist to be above us, but rather with us.

The next time you pray, I suggest you look up, feel up, be up, with your spirit and His spirit meeting together. Don't apologize for being God's own creation.

## This One Is for You

Many times speeches or talks are given to a group of people both large and small. A lot of the time, the larger the crowd, the less people focus and listen. The feeling is "this is for a group and not for the individual." You as the individual have a respectful responsibility to listen intently and receive the word to evaluate and consider. I have been doing this my entire life and am amazed at how much I have learned and also how much I needed to discard. Strive to have the ability to retain the truth and release the delusions that both exist in some presentations. There is a profound and opportune reason for being present at any meeting or gathering that we are required to be at, or that we choose to attend. Now, this same concept can and does apply to individual conversations we have with others daily. Be a catcher for the verbal exchanges that are thrown to you. Once you have the ball, you can decide which direction it needs to go.

## Journey

Each day as we leave our homes, it is a journey or trip. We always have plans for this day and hopefully they are accomplished to our satisfaction. So, as we return home each time, it may be good to evaluate how things went. Did we find the expected comfortable? How did we deal with the unexpected? These are questions I like to ask myself as I near the place I started from that day.

Likewise, our whole life is a journey that begins when we are born and ends when we take our last breath. When we near the end, how do we feel about the expected and unexpected events from our life? If you are reading this, you can still make changes in the direction you may seek. Each day is an opportunity to direct your path toward home in a meaningful manner. So that when you are very near home you can say to yourself, "Well done, good and faithful servant."

# 3 | I Do Declare

## Dying Day

We all know we face this day from the very moment we are born. Yet, very few people want to talk about or discuss this event in time. Some of the responses are: "Why should I? There isn't anything I can do about it anyway. It will happen when it happens. Why worry about it? I am going to enjoy every day of life given to me."

When we plan a physical trip, we make many preparations, such as mode of travel, rooms or housing on arrival, new wardrobe of clothing so we look our best. We make sure we have enough finances to pay for the trip. Why not make plans for a spiritual trip, which is what our dying day is?

We may do this by living a loving, kind, compassionate, generous, and mutual daily life. Think about this occasionally, and assess whether you are going in the right direction, with enough spiritual finances to encourage many hearts and souls to follow the path to eternal happiness and joy.

When John Wooden, the famous UCLA basketball coach, was on his deathbed at nearly 100 years old, his close friend asked him if he was afraid of dying. His reply was, "Some years ago, I would have said yes, but now I know this day will be the most beautiful day of my life. Why be afraid?"

## Could It Be

They called it global warming.
Said it is very alarming.
The ice is melting, flooding is near.
How will Earth survive another year?
Oh, the planet is getting so hot
Seems all these reports are from where we are not.
Nature has and always will
A balance to keep going still.
People with small and fearful minds
Promote fear and anxiety of all kinds.
Take care of our Earth as best we can.
Use care and thought to protect our land.
Please don't tell me the sky is falling.
Leave Chicken Little to do that calling.
Could it be there is a selfish motive
For all the pretenders who profit when they give
The sound of the alarm to all the masses?
I see the liars as a bunch of asses.

## Homeless

This word "homeless" is heard often in our society today. Did you ever think about the meaning of this word? There are a variety of descriptions given by people when asked the meaning. The obvious one is someone who lacks a house or structure to live in, and is begging for food on the street. Of course, that is materially accurate. Another will say it is someone who isn't part of a traditional family with parents and siblings and extended relatives. Another would be someone who doesn't belong to a team or club or some organization. I believe the homeless are the many of the world's population who don't have somebody who has opened their arms and hearts to them. There is a home inside all of us which we can find and share with as many as we choose to. It is vital to find the home in us that is resided in by our Creator before we can open it and share it with all mankind. We will not find it by looking to all the magnificent buildings and furnishings of our material desires. These are totally empty of what a real home is. It is the love that many homeless still crave, until welcomed by one of us, through Him.

## Generosity

We try and we try
And we don't get high
Enough for the people who on us depend.
They use all the energy we have to spend.
Don't they see the totality we give?
Please leave us something on which to live
So we can multiply our gifts
To over and over and over give lifts
To those we love and to those we share.
Because if it's all gone, there is no more there.

## Greed and Speed

Ten years ago, I coined the phrase, "Greed and Speed." It described the mentality and habits of our society at the time. "Get all I can and as fast as I can." It didn't matter who would get hurt. Most people scoffed and ridiculed my phrase as being skeptical and cynical. Well, unfortunately, it progressed to the present time in magnificent fashion. Now I am hearing, "Remember that phrase you used some years back? You were right." Sad to say, our society has suffered greatly along the way. The crash of the economy in 2008–2009 was a direct result of the housing financing fiasco of buying houses with no money down, and sometimes no job, also the reselling of the loans. Wall Street corruption and market manipulation led to many losses, especially in the commodities, when trading was not based on value, only the sleight of hand using the computer. Bankruptcies, huge companies going under, and personal credit card accounts became uncollectible. Bailouts, blame, and finger pointing are rampant. Restructuring and regulations hope to make a difference, but we will have to wait and see if people will let go of their greed, or are planning to rebound with it.

## Politics

Some are on the left, some on the right.
It seems all they do is verbally fight.
They do it with so much might
That the issues on tap, they lose sight.
Why are some so dense
And others on the fence?
Please focus with a clear lens
And use what is left of common sense.
Elections come and elections go.
Candidates all want you to believe they know
Why the quality of life advances so slow.
Just vote for me and I will show.
Divisions cause the ups and downs
Till a new group comes to Washington.
A group where within, Truth wears the crown
Will do great things and be in history's renown.

## Social Justice

The most discussed topic within the Catholic Church at present is striving for social justice, and ending poverty. These are noble and worthwhile goals, but I'm doubting the approach is accurate or successful. I believe we are looking at solutions through man's eyes and not God's Spirit.

To recall St. Paul in a very meaningful quote: "Those who have much, do not have more, and those who have little, do not have less." God does not discriminate in providing for all mankind with enough for a fulfilled life. This spiritual aspect is constantly being overlooked. What and who gets in the way of God's provisions? Human beings with cruel and destructive behavior, such as ethnic cleansing, interception of supplies for starving people, and downright and absolute hatred and bitterness toward their fellow man.

How do these people continue their power? In many ways visible and not so visible. Who is selling these dictators arms and profit so they can purchase huge destructive materials? Possibly, it is many of the companies in the so-called free world, who make huge profits from the arms and materials sales, and rape the countryside of raw materials from these poor countries: materials such as diamonds, gold, oil, and lots of valuable commodities in today's marketplace. These goods could purchase the end to material poverty in vast areas if the local or native people were permitted to participate.

Let's examine how many convents, colleges, dioceses and individuals have investments in many of these profitable endeavors, sometimes "hidden" within mutual funds and investment portfolios. With the Internet, one would think that this information could be discovered quite easily. If so, Mea culpa, mea culpa, mea maxima culpa.

Let us identify and call out these companies and their unjust practices. The owners of these investments could also sell these properties and use the proceeds to educate the world about it. The Catholic Church has had in the past, and still has, a powerful voice in the world, if, of course, it chooses to use it. The Church's direction against injustice is sometimes minimal and passive. In giving help, I would offer that it is difficult to give justice to someone, but rather one should work on stopping and diminishing injustice.

Ever since grade school until the present, people have been taught how to fundraise, and measure their success as to the amounts solicited. I doubt very much that Jesus did any fundraising when He lived on Earth. Instead He taught and converted people's minds and hearts to kindness, compassion, but most of all to love.

So, I feel we are missing the core application of social justice and ending poverty. I suggest to focus once again on St. Paul's resounding observation: "Those who have much do not have more, and those who have little do not have less." Let us put an end to the spiritual poverty many of us are experiencing in life, and speak out much clearer, and louder, and often, about the big picture of greed and corruption that most of us are involved in, in some way, through material connection, and sometimes tacit approval by our silence. If we who are seeking social justice can solve spiritual poverty, the solution to economic and material poverty will follow hastily.

Another subject that is strongly related to social justice is the allowance of abortion on demand in this country as well as others. How in God's beautiful creation can anything resembling justice be carried out in ending the life of an unborn child? This is the most hypocritical scenario that can be imagined, and yet, we as a church community vote for people in public office who agree and even champion this despicable act over and over and over again. Many of these people in office are members in good standing of the Catholic Church. Is it any surprise the abortion proponent candidate carried the Catholic vote for presidency in 2008? And yet the rhetoric continues, and the platitudes about being judgmental flow, but justice is nowhere in sight. Speak out clearly, speak out loudly, and speak out often for the life that has no voice. This will be an act of real social justice.

## Inspiration

After lots of deliberation
I am searching for inspiration.
Each day, as I look around
There isn't very much to be found.
People expect something from everyone they meet
When it's the giving of what you have that is neat.
This may be your talents, as well as material stuff.
Many times, even a little turns out to be enough.
Role models are needed, especially for our youth
As they get old enough for the voting booth.
Sharing your wisdom and knowledge
Can educate in addition to college.
So I'm asking all of you to co-conspire
In sharing your gifts for good, and indeed inspire.

## Religion

Organized religions often set rigid tests of self. They teach us what not to do instead of what we should do. What a dilemma for young people at a developing age. And lo and behold, these habits of decision making and false conscience forming lead to habits and traditions that often last for a lifetime. And, in a flash, we become older, and old, and these conflicts are still with many of us. The truth shall set us free!

For many years, Churches acted in a protectionist fashion. They can't tell the people everything they know for they may lose their attention and support. So, let's keep them fearful and obedient, and promise them salvation. Salvation is not the Churches to give, but rather it is a God given right as a child of God, for us to reclaim by living a Christ-like life. Jesus said "whoever *sees* me and believes in me will be saved." Many do not see the real, authentic, Jesus; and yet profess to believe in him. Jesus' teaching, sacrificing, and resurrection were actually lived for us to *see*, and not offered to us as a story to be heard.

The years of these practices are finally changing in many of these churches, but change has not yet been reached. In my own Catholic Faith, far too many of the younger generation are still at arm's length, and not totally embraced. Instead, they are met by the cold aspect of the old and rigid rules of traditional Catholicism. The age of evangelization needs to explore the communication of the Internet as well as gathering in the churches. People need to feel welcome and understood in their journey into spirituality.

The Church is a tremendous support community, and certainly should not be abandoned. As a life-long Catholic, I have seen both the old and the new and, unfortunately, I see many lost in the desert in both ages. Our last several popes have been tremendous in their teachings. Too bad many of us chose not to listen to them. We tie their positions to the past failures of many before them. We definitely need more role models and leaders in the Church, at many of the local levels as well. Also we need more spiritual authors and more thoughtful readers. I personally have learned, or at least had confirmed, many of my present awakenings through reading.

## Thirst

During a recent conversation, one man talked about having a water barrel in his backyard. It was recessed and heated to provide drinking water for all the friendly wild animals in his area. He said as the winter advanced, the number of partakers increased. I found this to be a parallel to our spiritual thirst, and our finding the reservoir to provide fulfillment. As our environment reduces access to fluids, we search for other ways to find them. I feel our thirst or yearning for the waters of understanding and light is continuous as we learn and drink from them. Our human bodies require sufficient hydration to perform as a satisfactory level and to maintain good health. Likewise, our spiritual health and energy need to be nourished by the waters of nature and Love. Don't be afraid or apprehensive to look for this need in unusual or new places where it is offered. Always explore the path and the unknown where your thirst often takes you. Do not deny your thirst or your ability to quench it.

## Exploration

I heard the comment from an older person, "I don't want to try the new because the old way was good enough this far, and I don't have many years left." I believe exploring a new way to see if it offers us a fuller or more complete way to live is very wise and beneficial. My use of the word "way" in this discussion is meant to point to a way of thinking and feeling and learning. Many people are content with their religious beliefs and other structures of religion. I do not say this is wrong, but rather I believe they are limited. Our beliefs shouldn't be based solely on family and community tradition. This is often the reason people cling to them as a shield. "If it was good enough for them, it is good enough for me." Spirituality is not something to be shielded or protected from. Instead, it is an eternal fountain and flame to be explored and nourished and enjoyed. To explore should not be to fear. One need not replace what one already has, but take an opportunity to build on or add to it. Scripture says, "The truth shall set you free." The light many of us are afraid to let shine is silently waiting for us to release. All it takes is the courage and willingness to begin exploring.

## The Why

When I was a youngster in school, I always hated the Why questions. The What, When, and Where were easy because this was always in the textbook. The Why was and is a mystery. Mysteries are always hard to answer. This is why we need to reduce or eliminate the mysteries of life. Mysteries disappear when answers appear. Life is simple, life is natural, life is transparent. The reason a mystery is difficult or hard to see or understand is our obstruction to reality and truth. The curse is, if we don't like what's there, we can get around or change it and call it a mystery. We seem to want to have the flexibility to have our way, and often at any cost.

So, let us answer the question of "why". Why do we exist, why do we make the daily choices we make, why do we put ourselves in many cases ahead of others? Every individual needs to answer these questions themselves. I believe I exist to Live, Love and Learn. Now to what degree I do these three things will determine the degree of my reward. I believe the level of reward is unlimited because our Creator and our creation are unlimited. Why are we here, Why are we challenged, Why are we gifted, Why are we searching, Why are we yearning? The answer is to reach Oneness where everything resides.

## A Bargain

Our secular society has become obsessed with the search for a bargain. We look for bargains anytime we purchase something. We shop for cars, homes, clothing, everyday things (yes, even toothpaste). We look endlessly for ways to receive discounts from the retail price. It has become so severe with some people, they will not purchase anything unless it is considered a bargain. People begin living their lives at a bargain rate. Life is given to us at full value so there is no need to compromise, haggle, or barter with it. And yet our mentality and habits lead us to "bargain" by making excuses, casting blame, and rationalizing. All this is done in order to make a deal, and usually get an advantage over another. Many are then satisfied and content knowing they made a good bargain. We are all given full value in life and it appears in various abilities and dimensions in different people. It is our task and to our benefit to search and see the equally full value of each person. It diminishes our own lives when we compete for and look for a fault or defect to exploit. There are no faults or defects in the lives we were given, only those that we ourselves create. Live life to the full value you were given!

## Transformation

Webster says to "transform" is to change in structure, appearance, or character. Someone might say it means to put off the old and put on the new. I believe it means to change our attitude or approach to life. If this changes, so does our behavior and hopefully our character. Our character consists of many core principles. Some of these are honesty, integrity, compassion, humility, trust, sense of justice, responsibility, and commitment. People often try to transform others with advice, manipulation, coaxing, and intimidation. This usually has a disappointing result. It is up to each one of us to examine our need for transformation and act accordingly. Some of us need a sudden and dramatic act such as St. Paul being struck down off his horse. Others may only need to tweak their behavior and outlook to feel new and be new. Progress is made when we transform ourselves. My first grade teacher taught us a simple saying: "Good, Better, Best. Never let it rest. Until the Good is Better and the Better Best." Let us all strive to be "the best we can be."

## Message to the World

The first words that come to mind are from a Burt Bacharach song from the 70s: "What the world needs now, is love, sweet love. That's the only thing we have just too little of." It is a sad situation in the world that, when you say to another, "I love you," unless you are a spouse or a parent or a child, people become very defensive and skeptical. The feeling, "They must want something from me," when the very opposite is true. The person wants to give something, the most valuable gift one has, the offering of love. Let us put honesty and sincerity in our feelings and words so that the reception of them will be much greater. Whether we agree or not, we all came into this world through an act of love. Love is the prerequisite of happiness. Love is the seed and the nourishment of a happy life in this world. Happiness is not a right or a guarantee, but rather an opportunity, and also a challenge to learn and experience the awesome result it offers us. Love is not offered to us as an object, but instead a way of relating to our fellow human beings, as well as our Creator.

Our actions currently trigger what we offer to others, as well as what we receive. This concept of reality is not meant to be a competition between ourselves and everyone else. Many of us live our lives as exclusive, and not inclusive, which leads to a degree of unhappiness and lack of fulfillment. Use the power and might of love to influence everyone you come in contact with. Love is eternally contagious. Love is where you need to go to improve the lives of everyone.

Another virtue that is in enormous need is patience. When the attempt to live and learn love with kindness and compassion fails to elicit the desired response, it is a natural response to become impatient and frustrated. The fact remains, love didn't fail, only the refusal of the intended person to receive it. So this leads us to communicate and educate in an improved manner. Some people have the need to understand before allowing anything to come in, even love. The best teacher in this area is "example." It is much more effective than words and explanations. Patience also affords us the luxury to relax. People in today's rapidly changing world tend to be very uptight and tense about daily situations. This is not healthy or rewarding. So it is imperative to find a way of relaxing.

I also recommend learning from the experienced and wise people who surround us in life. Their advice and direction, when sought, is of immeasurable value. Become aware of the natural order of creation and how synchronized it all is. Awareness opens the door to the vast power and impact of the whole universe, and awards us the chance to allow it to work positively in our lives. We need to work at removing the obstacles or resistance to the light that nourishes each of us when we grasp it. When you get this far, prepare to enjoy the purpose of being given the gift of life. We now give the gift of love back to life in all of its forms.

My message is not advice on how to gain fame and fortune. It is not about economics, religious ideology, or coveted possessions. These things advance nothing more than an unending circle of want. Love supersedes all things—and I emphasize "all."

To quote the Sufi poet Rumi:

> And don't look for me in human shape. I am inside your looking.
> No room for form with love this strong. Beat the drum, let the poets speak.
> This is a day of purification for those who are already mature and initiated into what love is.
> No need to wait until we die.
> There's more to want here than money and being famous and bites of roasted meat.

Joe Sigwarth and his daughter Virginia.

# 4. Poetic Lines to Loves of Mine

## Where Else?

There is a place that is known as Balltown.
As places go, it is a very small town.
But it has everything there you need.
Just stop in at Skip Breitbach's Feed.
Skip serves the surrounding area.
At times, it becomes close to hysteria.
The busy season is in the Spring, for seed.
Everyone needs it right now in order to succeed.
The boss is always there, from early morning till night.
If there is anything wrong, he will make it right.
He sells Big Gain products to most of the dairies.
Of course the preferred way is cash and carry.
He sells flowers, plants, and antiques.
Anything and everything that is unique.
A high volume business for a town this size.
Skip calls the place a "Slice of Paradise."

## Best Food In Town

There is an establishment that is brightly shining.
The name of it is Breitbach's Country Dining.
The food prepared and served is exceptional and hearty.
There is no better place for a dinner party.
The only thing that could exceed the quality of food
Is the people who greet you and serve you so good.
Mike, Cindy, family, and all the rest
Make this place the absolute best.
They received the James Beard Award in 2008.
This is a national acclaim that is quite great.
Traveled to New York, and in front of a big crowd
Made the small town of Balltown humbly proud.
So I will say once again, the only thing that tops the food quality
Is the tremendous brand of hospitality.
Please stop in and enjoy the food and drink.
And when you return home tell people what you think
Of this oasis in the desert of big restaurants
Gives you the warmth of home and leaves nothing to want.

## Bill

Happy Birthday, Bill, at year sixty-five.
After Mayo, it's great to be alive.
But you are alive in so many ways
With a loving heart that forever stays.
As you learn many of life's answers
You become a more complete dancer
With the people who give you love.
I assure you I am one of the above.
Let us celebrate who we are.
I see you as a bright, bright star
Sent by God to show us His Light
To each of us who see it and enjoy with delight.
My wish for you is joy and happiness
As you receive our love's caress.

## Madeline

Is she a diamond or a pearl?
She is such a beautiful girl.
I would say she is much, much more
For her life has wondrous things in store.
We get tired of things that we wear
But the beauty of this child will always be there.
The genuine innocence of this girl of two
Makes us all feel like we are brand new.
Her actions happen to teach us a lot.
Things we have lived but now have forgot.
So if you like jewels that really shine
We have one here in this grandchild of mine.

## Life on a Dairy Farm

Five a.m., time to start the day.
What lies ahead who can say.
Some surprises come our way.
To start, we milk the cows, and feed them hay.
Next it's time to clean the barn.
The cows are outside till it gets warm.
No need to sound the alarm.
Everything is fine, there is no harm.
Now into the barn they file.
Time to relax and rest for awhile.
To lie in comfort and digest.
This makes for a high milk test.
Next is time to feed some more.
Or if you need to, go to the store.
Also grab a bite of lunch before
It is time for sure to milk and chore.
That means there are calves to feed.
Maybe a newborn with extra need.
There are also other efforts to succeed.

Some are even taught to lead.
For prevention of ills, we vaccinate.
For reproduction, we inseminate.
On these procedures you can't be late
Or the outcome won't be so great.
There is always something to do on a dairy.
The schedule of 24–7 is scary.
But farmers continue to carry on
Because without them, where would milk come from?

## Joseph

It is ten years ago today
When young Joseph left us, could not stay.
Only in bodily form did he leave
So there isn't any need to grieve.
We shall not be bitter with scorn.
His small body was injured and worn.
Where he went, we shall also be.
His spirit is here for us all to see.
His love lives on and is embraced
As three more children were given in this case
To the family that continues to grow
In a large way because of little Joe.

## Dependence

When your car lets you down
On your face appears a frown.
Now why did this happen to me?
I'm in a hurry, don't you see.
You have always been here for me before.
All I ask is just start up once more.
I know it's because you're not feeling good.
You are asking me to look under the hood.
I won't know what to do if I take a look.
I suppose I could peek in your book.
I won't be able to fix why you're stuck.
I think I'll call the Triple A truck.
He will get you going, and once again I'll depend
On you serving me to a happy end.

## Quinn's Baptism Day

Welcome to this special occasion
When, for me, you all have high expectations.
I do promise these to fulfill
If your values in me you instill.
I will do this, not as a test
But working as a team with the best.
To love and be loved is all I ask.
This challenge is also your task.
Thank you to my Creator and co-creators
And to you who are gathered here—there's nothing greater.
I came here with a divine mission.
So I pray for the wisdom to always listen.
Thanks for being here with me today
To give me a strong start on my way.
I feel the warmth and energy abound.
Let's celebrate with good food and a round.

## Wonder

My time is here, my time is now.
So what am I doing milking a cow?
Many more important things to do.
Life has become too much like an old shoe.
The same routine, with little reward.
It is today that I should be looking toward.
I can love, care, and speak, and do some good
But most often, I am not understood.
The days I have left shall not be wasted.
Instead, the good life shall be tasted.
Helping and loving others will be my employ.
Finding ways to spread the joy.
So as I sit here under a cow and ponder.
When will this arrive—this land of wonder?

## Herb

Herb has arrived at 70 years of age.
Still has a lot left in his fuel gauge.
We all gather to celebrate.
Of course, being Sigwarths, none of us is late.
Herb and Cheryl's family, so healthy and strong.
We hope all of their lives will be quite long
To enjoy the friendship and love of each other
And also reflect the lives of father and mother.
So grab a drink of your choice.
Let us all loudly rejoice.
Use your own pick of a verb
To sing Happy Birthday to Herb.

## Bridget, Worthy of Praise

Congratulations, Bridget, you've come so far.
You have become like a bright shining star.
Live for today in everything you do.
Yesterday is gone, so start over new.
You've confirmed your love and faith in Jesus.
Don't forget Him, because He also needs us
To become aware as we work and grow.
Remember to accept His will and never say no.
For His Love and Guidance will make you strong
Each and every day as your life goes along.
Give thanks to God and family for where you are
And continue on your path, and go as far as your star.

## Gerti, A Birthday Wish

On a happy birthday for Gerti.
You are 88 and still pretty.
You are still on the go, go go.
You are not even getting slow.
No regrets and at peace with yourself.
You are not ready to go on the shelf.
May days for you to enjoy be more.
Who knows what goodness is still in store?
So give thanks for friends and family.
To God and parents especially.
Your trials and blessings have been many.
Showing them both to you in Francis and Denny.
But on you go to another day
To give your help in some way.
Stay strong as you are and trust in the Lord
And happiness will be your eternal reward.

## My Brother and Friend

I just looked at a photo of years past.
My brother is in it and very picturesque.
He is sitting upon a horse he knew.
Francis always said horses give back to you.
He looked puzzled and lonely at this time.
A large family and heritage was fine.
His question was, "Do you love me," of course.
The only one who answered "yes" was the horse.

## Kristiana Is Here

She came a bit late.
She brought lots of cheer.
We no longer need to wait.
Kristiana is here.
She burst into life with a new start
With love to receive and love to give.
I assure you she has a warm heart
And a very beautiful future to live.
She is blessed with two wonderful parents
Who will do their part as life unfolds
And of course also the grandparents.
With strength and wisdom worth a ton of gold
Her life's door is opened wide.
For this we are thankful to the Lord.
Let us rejoice to coincide
And shout Hooray and Alleluia with one accord.


## A Child Is Born

Oh what joy.
It's a boy.
Call came on line.
He is so very fine.
Time to give thanks.
Another child joins the ranks.
Grandpa says relax, pull up a chair.
Oh, no, too much excitement in the air.
Years ago 'twas whiskey and cigars came out.
Today high fives, fist bumps, and a shout.
When a child comes along
It's time to write a song.
A lullaby would make him coo.
But for me, a poem will have to do.

## Cosmic Beauty of "O" Show

How do I describe this beauty just right?
More than the stars that shine at night.
The coordination, the music, the energy comes together
To perform an event absolutely like none other.
To see God's human creatures present this gift
Gives all who witness it a fantastic lift.
People flock from all over the world
To see this masterpiece unfurled.
I give thanks to the Lord above.
This event the audience will forever love.
This performance is both nuclear and sublime.
The description that fits it best is Divine.

## Milly

Another birthday and here we go again.
The third in our family to become an octogenarian.
We are here to celebrate all about Milly.
Her many jokes may cause us to act silly.
Her beautiful voice can carry a song.
As children, we listened to her singing all day long.
Her fingers and thread and sewing machine
No one is better at sewing a seam.
She remains independent with her health and ability
And lives life with utmost sensibility.
As friends and family gather today,
We all with heartfelt thought would like to say,
We love you Milly, and with God's help you'll stay
Happy and healthy until your centenary birthday.

## December Hello

She came out of the Northeast.
As storms go, she was a beast.
First came the snow, over 15 inches.
Then the wind started blowing, filling the ditches.
The sub-zero cold was next to come.
How I wish this storm was done.
Maybe tomorrow the sun will shine
And life will be more sublime.
Not too many of these, I pray.
Although it is early, and here to stay.
Give me Summer, Fall, and Spring
As Winter makes me forget everything
About the nice weather the rest of the year.
If I could give back winter, I wouldn't shed a tear.


## Irene, All Saints Birthday, November 1st

Another year of life and service
And you've done it without being nervous.
We're all so happy you have contentment and peace
With these your blessings will surely increase.
Getting older isn't so bad
As long as you are happy and glad
For the years you have given so well.
You take care of everything, we can tell.
You are so great at the family history.
You only tell the good and the glory.
When a family gathering is to be
You will come for all to see.
To show the love for all you share
And how much you really care.
The mood from your family is grateful and serene.
We all say thanks, and Happy Birthday, dear Irene.

## Wade, a Daddy

Who holds the strength of an old oak tree
There to bounce you on his knee?
Has time to play with you with glee
Showing love for all to see?
Shows you how to be steady
So you don't get too heady?
Makes sure you're always ready?
The one, of course, we call Daddy.
There is one who lives in Prior Lake
Who can cook, and even bake.
He is real, he is not a fake.
He is a fine one our God did make.
A family foundation he has made
With heart and soul has carefully laid.
He is the one we wouldn't trade.
He is our most wonderful Wade.

## Divine Intervention

Two people met forty years ago
For the very first time, you know.
This was called a blind date.
It was the beginning of each one's fate.
It was love at first sight.
They each seemed so right.
Sharing the love brought a family to become
Five grown children is the sum.
The next generation is already started.
Thirteen so far, of which one is departed.
Life has flourished for these first two.
But now there is the question, "What to do?"
Of course, to enjoy the family so bright.
They surely are their delight.
May the next forty years be as kind

For all who are involved in heart and mind.
The future started at that first greeting.
May the pulse continue to keep on beating.

## Mother-in-Law

There are many who are very kind,
Yet lots of these are much maligned.
The ones I've seen are good indeed.
They seem to show up when there is need.
My very own was truly a saint.
She knew when to show restraint.
I loved her as much as I possibly could.
She loved me also, I was sure she would.
When problems arose, she was there
With wisdom and action to help repair.
What I see is such great attitude
And seldom do I show enough gratitude.
At dinnertime a meal would appear.
This is why we hold her dear.
Thoughtfulness and kindness does flourish
As our family she helped nourish.
Always doing whatever she can.
After all, she is Grandma to our children.

## The Plane

The enormous bird that flies so high
At 30,000 feet up in the sky.
No matter how I spin it
Today I'm sure glad I'm in it.

## Take It Easy

Everyone says to Joe, "Relax,"
When all around us is going the max.
If I allow my work to go lax
Won't have enough to pay the tax.
Relax is such an easy word to repeat
For people who can't stand the heat.
To always go slow would be neat
But not when passion draws the elite.
There are those who always get the job done
Before the setting of the sun.
If there is any time left for some fun,
How about a nice long run?
Always thought going easy was for the old
But guess what I'm being told?
It is time for me to join the fold.
I'm told, "Take a rest, you're precious as gold."
Stay awhile and each morn feel the dew.
As each day starts anew
I've decided this is something I must do.
But how to start, I haven't a clue.

## Backache

The pain in my back is giving me fits.
Time to see physical therapy for some new twists.
Bend this way and twist that
Mostly done while lying flat.
Seems like a lot of work to feel good.
This part I've never quite understood.
Maybe it's from issues I have inside.
Who'd think that would coincide?
So as I heal within, as well as out,
I learn more good solutions to tout.
About creation's chaotic harmony
Played as a classical symphony.

## Truth

Oh, if only we can control
Our mind and ego.
Because it is in our inner self soul
Where we find the Know.

## Magic of Maui

September 17, 2011, was a day of renown.
Hundreds of people descended on Balltown.
A Holstein cow sale was the event.
It was held under a large special tent.
Many people came to bid.
Some lots blew off the lid.
The effort and work to make it go
Paid off with a magnificent show.
It was the end of a successful career
By a family that holds cows dear.
When they all finally leave the farm
With memories that turn into yarn
It is time to relax and reflect
For the twilight years need to connect.
Many ask me what I will do.
I'll live a life that is thoughtful and true.
To give everyone an encore to the event
That was held under that special tent.

# Final Words

Thank you for being interested in reading the words and thoughts on these pages. My intent is to provoke thoughts in order to give you answers in life. After all, this is where answers lie—within us. Perhaps it will also provoke conversation as we go forward in life. I also hope that you had a smile or laugh at some of the poems. I enjoyed meeting you by doing these writings, and will enjoy that relationship always.

Love, Joe